READER'S DIGEST

GREAT**HEALTHY**COOKING

Perfect Poultry

READER'S DIGEST

GREAT HEALTHY COOKING

Perfect Poultry

Reader's
Digest

THE READER'S DIGEST ASSOCIATION, INC.
Pleasantville, New York/Montreal

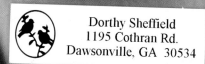

PERFECT POULTRY is part of a cookbook series called
GREAT HEALTHY COOKING.

Editorial Director: Carol A. Guasti
Design Director: Elizabeth Tunnicliffe
Produced by: Beth Allen Associates, Inc.
  President/Editorial Director: Beth Allen
  Art Director: Kathleen McGilvery
  Nutritionist: Michele C. Fisher, Ph.D., R.D.
  Recipe Tester: Lorna Charles
  Copy Editor: Wendy Marcus
Photographers: Sue Atkinson, Martin Brigdale, Gus Filgate, Graham Kirk
Stylists: Sue Russell, Helen Trent

Reader's Digest General Books
Editor-in-Chief: Christopher Cavanaugh
Art Director: Joan Mazzeo

Reader's Digest General Books/United Kingdom
Editorial Director: Cortina Butler
Art Director: Nick Clark
Series Editor: Christine Noble

Library of Congress Cataloging in Publication Data
Perfect Poultry.
     p.   cm.--(Reader's Digest great healthy cooking)
   Includes index.
   ISBN 0-7621-0275-6
   1. Cookery (Poultry)   I. Reader's Digest Association.
   II. Series.
   TX750.P4697   1999
   641.6'6—dc21   99-44148

First Edition Copyright © 1999
The Reader's Digest Association Limited
11 Westferry Circus, Canary Wharf, London E14 4HE

Copyright © 1999 The Reader's Digest Association, Inc.
Copyright © 1999 The Reader's Digest Association (Canada) Ltd.
Copyright © 1999 Reader's Digest Association Far East Limited
Philippine Copyright © 1999 Reader's Digest Association Far East Limited

Printed in the United States of America 1999

Notes to the reader
• Recipes were tested using standard measurements by
  professional recipe testers, to ensure perfect results.
• Conventional ovens, not convection or microwave ovens,
  were used in the kitchen testing of recipes.
• Large eggs were used.
• Low-fat milk (2% milkfat) was used unless another is specified.
• Can sizes are approximate, as weights can vary slightly
  according to the manufacturer.
• Preparation and cooking times are intended only as a guide.

The nutritional information in this book is for reference only.
Anyone with continuing medical problems or symptoms should
consult a doctor.

Contents

6

Introduction
Eating well to live well

8

Versatile Poultry

26

Beginnings

42
Sensational Salads

62
Poultry in a Hurry

78
Main Course Poultry

122
Super Sandwiches

Eating well to live well

It's no secret: Eating a healthful diet and leading a health-filled lifestyle help you look good, feel great, and have lots of energy. Nutrition fads come and go. But it's a fact that eating well for your health's sake is simple. Eat a variety of foods, because no one food contains all the vitamins, minerals, fiber, and other essential nutrients you need. And get the balance right. This means look at the overall picture of which foods you eat, when you eat them, and how much you eat. And be sure to get exercise along the way.

Getting the balance right!

The Dietary Guidelines for Americans help us to get the balance right by eating a healthy diet. The United States Department of Agriculture (USDA) and the Department of Health and Human Services used the most current scientific information available to develop these guidelines for all Americans (age 2 or older). By following these guidelines, you not only can enjoy better health, but also can reduce your chances for getting certain diseases.

The Dietary Guidelines for Americans

1. *Eat a variety of foods* to get the energy, protein, vitamins, minerals, and fiber you need for good health.
2. *Balance the food you eat with physical activity — maintain or improve your weight* to reduce your chances of high blood pressure, heart disease, certain cancers, and a stroke.
3. *Choose a diet with plenty of grain products, vegetables, and fruits* that provide needed vitamins, minerals, fiber, and complex carbohydrates, and that can help you lower your intake of fat.
4. *Chose a diet low in fat, saturated fat, and cholesterol* to reduce your risk of heart attack and certain types of cancer and to help you maintain a healthy weight.
5. *Choose a diet moderate in sugars.* A high-sugar diet has too many calories and too few nutrients for most people and can contribute to tooth decay. Use that "spoonful of sugar" sparingly!
6. *Choose a diet moderate in salt and sodium* (no more than 2,400mg each day) to help reduce your risk of high blood pressure.
7. *If you drink alcoholic beverages, do so in moderation* (no more than 1 to 2 drinks a day). Alcoholic beverages supply calories but little or no nutrients. Drinking is also the cause of many health problems and accidents, and can lead to addiction.

Putting the Dietary Guidelines into action

By following the Food Guide Pyramid, you put the Dietary Guidelines for Americans into daily action. The Pyramid calls for eating a variety of foods to get the nutrients you need to maintain your health. It's designed to guide you toward a diet that does not have too many calories or too much fat, saturated fat, cholesterol, sugar, sodium, and alcohol. Such a low-fat diet reduces your chances of getting certain diseases and helps you maintain a healthy weight.

The Food Guide Pyramid

The Pyramid (opposite) is an outline of what to eat each day. It's not a rigid prescription but a general guide that lets you choose a healthful diet that's right for you. By eating the suggested servings from each food group each day, you'll be enjoying a diet that not only gives you the nutrients you need, but at the same time, the right amount of calories to maintain or improve your weight. You'll also be following a diet that helps you keep your intake of fats and saturated fats low. This is important, because most American diets are too high in fat, especially saturated fat.

The five major food groups in the Pyramid (the three lower sections) are needed for good health. No one food group is more important than another — for good health you need them all! Each of the food groups provides some but not all of the nutrients you need. Foods in one food group cannot replace those in another.

How many calories do you need each day?

The Pyramid shows a range of servings for each major food group. The number of servings that are right for you depends on how many calories you need — based on your age, sex, size, and your lifestyle, that is, how active you are. Almost everyone should have at least the minimum number of servings listed for each group.

Here are three calorie level suggestions, based upon recommendations of the National Academy of Sciences and on calorie intakes reported in national food consumption surveys.

1,600 Calories—	appropriate for many sedentary women and some older adults
2,200 Calories—	appropriate for most children, teenage girls, active women, and many sedentary men (pregnant and breastfeeding women may need more calories)
2,800 Calories —	appropriate for teenage boys, many active men, and some very active women

A day's sample diet

	1,600 Calories	2,200 Calories	2,800 Calories
Grain Group	6 servings	9 servings	11 servings
Vegetable Group	3 servings	4 servings	5 servings
Fruit Group	2 servings	3 servings	4 servings
Milk Group	2 to 3 servings*	2 to 3 servings*	2 to 3 servings*
Meat Group (ounces)	5 servings	6 servings	7 servings
Total Fat Grams	53	73	93
Total Added Sugars	6 teaspoons	12 teaspoons	18 teaspoons

* Women who are pregnant or breastfeeding, teenagers, and young adults to age 24 need 3 servings.

The Food Guide Pyramid
A Guide to Daily Food Choices

Fats, Oils & Sweets
Use Sparingly

Milk, Yogurt & Cheese
2-3 Servings

Meat, Poultry, Fish, Dry Beans, Eggs, & Nuts
2-3 Servings

Fruit Group
2-4 Servings

Vegetable Group
3-5 Servings

Bread, Cereals, Rice, & Pasta Group
6-11 Servings

The Food Groups

Breads, cereals, rice, and pasta — eat 6 to 11 servings a day

At the base of the Pyramid are foods from grains — breads, cereals, rice, and pasta. These foods provide complex carbohydrates, which are an important source of energy, especially in low-fat diets. They also provide vitamins, especially those from the B group, as well as many minerals and fiber. Choose foods made from whole grains whenever possible. They contain fiber that helps prevent constipation and helps keep our digestive system healthy. Eat foods in this group made with little fat or sugars more often, such as English muffins, bread, and pasta. Go ahead, enjoy croissants, cakes, cookies, and pastries — but not often, as they are high in both fats and sugars.

Vegetables — eat 3 to 5 servings each day

Nutrition experts agree: Vegetables are low in fat, are good sources of fiber, and are good for us. Many vegetables are rich in antioxidant nutrients, vitamin C, and beta-carotene (which the body converts to vitamin A). They also contain phytochemical compounds that have been linked to reducing the risk of certain diseases, such as heart disease and cancer. They are also low in fat and provide fiber.

Fruits — eat 2 to 4 servings each day

Fruits are fabulous —in flavor and nutrition. Both fruits and fruit juices provide important amounts of vitamins A and C, potassium, and fiber too. Choose from fresh fruits, fruit juices (without added sugar), frozen, canned (in juice, not heavy syrups), and dried fruits. Eat whole fruits often, as they are higher in fiber than fruit juices. Citrus fruits, some melons, kiwis, and berries are especially high in vitamin C, so eat them often for immunity and healing.

Meats, poultry, fish, dry beans, eggs, and nuts — eat 2 to 3 servings each day

These high-protein foods provide protein for growth and cell repair, the B vitamins that help metabolize energy, iron which is needed to carry oxygen in the blood, and zinc which is necessary for growth and repair. The total number of 2 to 3 servings from this group equals 5 to 7 ounces of cooked lean meat, poultry, or fish each day, or equivalents of cooked dry beans, eggs, peanut butter, or nuts.

Milk, yogurt, and cheese — eat 2 to 3 servings each day

Dairy foods such as milk, yogurt, and cheese are the best source of calcium, needed for strong bones and teeth and to help prevent osteoporosis. They also provide vitamins such as riboflavin (B_2) and minerals. To keep the calories and fat intakes low, choose low-fat or skim milk, plus products made from them. Go easy on high-fat cheese and ice cream; look for low-fat cheeses and reduced-fat milk desserts, such as frozen ice milk and yogurt.

Fats, oils, and sweets — use sparingly

The Dietary Guidelines recommend that Americans limit fats in their diets to 30 percent of calories from fats. Fat contains more than twice as many calories per gram as either carbohydrates or proteins.

What's a serving?

Breads, cereals, rice, and pasta

1 slice of bread	1 ounce of ready-to-eat cereal	½ cup of cooked cereal, rice, or pasta

Vegetables

1 cup of raw leafy vegetables	½ cup of other vegetables cooked or chopped raw	¾ cup of vegetable juice

Fruits

1 medium apple, banana, orange	½ cup of chopped cooked, or canned fruit	¾ cup of fruit juice

Milk, yogurt, and cheese

1 cup of milk or yogurt	1½ ounces of natural cheese	2 ounces of processed cheese

Meats, poultry, fish, dry beans, eggs, and nuts

2 to 3 ounces of cooked lean meat, poultry, or fish	½ cup of cooked dry beans or 1 egg counts as 1 ounce of lean meat. 2 tablespoons of peanut butter or ⅓ cup of nuts counts as 1 ounce of lean meat

Recipe and Fruit Analyses

All recipes have been analyzed for their nutritional, vitamin, and mineral content, based upon the current USDA Nutrient Database for Standard Reference, using additional data from food manufacturers, where appropriate. The Daily Values, the standard values developed by the Food and Drug Administration (FDA) for use on food labels, were used to determine the following terms and symbols found throughout this book (see also pages 140 and 141):

✓✓✓   or excellent   at least 50% (half)

✓✓   or good   25% to 50% (one-quarter to one-half)

✓   or fair   10 to 25% (one-tenth to one-quarter)

V   denotes that a recipe is suitable for vegetarians.

Note: Recipes contribute other nutrients, but the analyses only include those that provide at least 10% of the Daily Value. Vitamins and minerals, when negligible, are not included.

Versatile Poultry

The ideal meal starter

START WITH POULTRY FOR THE PERFECT MEAL — whether you're mixing up a quick supper, planning a harvest celebration, packing a picnic, or just stacking up a sandwich. Poultry is the delicious, nutritious answer! It's high in protein, low in fat, filled with B vitamins, and has essential minerals, too. Poultry is even better for you when you team it up with fresh vegetables and fruits. First, begin with the basics for buying, cooking, and storing the various birds. Then simmer up a stock, create a hearty stew, grill some delicious kebabs, or stack up a super sandwich. You will soon be enjoying the many marvelous meals that begin with poultry.

Poultry in a healthy diet

Whatever your tastes, whatever your lifestyle, poultry fits in. It rates high in protein and niacin — an excellent duo for the basis of a healthful diet. Poultry is also versatile: Stuff a hen, roast a turkey, braise some drumsticks, or toss it into a salad. For health and variety, poultry is always a good menu choice.

Essential for life

Protein, the essential body-building nutrient, is needed by every cell in the body. Cells need protein for growth, for development, for maintenance, for repair. Protein is also important for producing enzymes, antibodies, and hormones — playing an essential role in digestion, immunity, and other body functions. Protein is made up of amino acids, which are compounds containing the four elements that are needed for life: carbon, hydrogen, oxygen, and nitrogen. Twenty amino acids are commonly found in plant and animal proteins. The human body only makes eleven of these; the rest of the nine, called essential amino acids, must come from the foods we eat. Animal protein — those found in meat, poultry, game and game birds, fish, milk, cheese, and eggs —contains all of the nine essential amino acids and are therefore known as *complete proteins*. Other sources of protein, such as cereals, legumes, nuts, and seeds, lack one or more of the essential amino acids, thus are called *incomplete proteins.*

Eat a small amount of complete protein foods daily, as your body does not store them for later use (extra protein that is not needed that day is usually stored as fat). Some protein foods, such as poultry, are excellent "building blocks" for delicious menus.

Quality, not quantity

High-protein foods provide both protein and zinc for growth and cell repair, the B vitamins that help metabolize energy, and iron needed to carry oxygen in the blood. Because protein foods are so essential, you might think that protein is the number one nutrient to eat. This is not the case. For the ideal balanced diet, only 10% to 12% of our daily calories should come from protein. The Food Guide Pyramid suggests 2 to 3 servings of high-protein foods a day; this equals 5 to 7 ounces of cooked lean meat, poultry, or fish each day, or the equivalents of cooked dry beans, eggs, peanut butter, or nuts. A 3-ounce cooked portion is equal to a medium-size boneless skinless chicken breast half.

Because you need only a small quantity of protein, quality counts! Choose lean poultry and game birds; they are a far better nutritional value for the money than high-fat products such as sausages, fatty meats, and pâtés. Poultry is a great alternative to other protein foods such as fatty red meats and full-fat cheeses.

▲ Removing the skin from chicken reduces the fat content considerably, even if this is done after cooking — the fat in chicken skin does not transfer to the meat during cooking.

versatile poultry

▲ The Food Guide Pyramid recommends 2 to 3 servings of protein foods each day. Here, a typical serving: a tender duck breast, roasted, then trimmed of its skin and any visible fat. It's served with a red currant sauce, plenty of potatoes (a starchy carbohydrate), and vitamin-rich vegetables.

Cutting the fat

Both chicken and turkey are particularly lean birds. Remove the skin, either before or after cooking, and you get even less fat. A 3-ounce chicken breast with the skin has 6.6 grams of fat. Remove the skin and you get only 3 grams of fat (less than 1 gram is saturated fat). That's less than half the fat!

Even duck has about the same amount of fat as lamb — provided you remove the skin and the fat before cooking. The meat of the duck is full of flavor, but quite lean.

Vitamins and minerals too

Poultry and game birds are important sources of B vitamins, including B_1 (thiamine), B_2 (riboflavin), niacin, B_6, and B_{12} — all essential for metabolizing foods into energy. They also provide many essential minerals such as zinc, iron, chromium, copper, selenium, phosphorus, potassium, and magnesium. Eating lean poultry and game birds is one of the easiest ways to ensure you get enough iron, zinc, and vitamin B_{12}. Chicken and turkey livers offer a lot of vitamin A, too.

Popular poultry

For versatility, flavor, and nutrition, poultry tops the list. Barbecue a chicken or roast a turkey. Stuff Cornish hens, grill some quail, or braise a capon. If you prefer rich dark meat, serve duck or goose. Whichever bird you choose, you'll be serving a meal filled with complete protein, vitamins, minerals, and great taste.

An ABC of poultry

To most people, poultry generally means just chicken and turkey. Poultry, by definition, is any domesticated bird used as food. Some have been considered wild birds, but now are often available in specialty meat markets and mail-order houses. Poultry includes such high-protein birds as chicken, duck, goose, guinea fowl, quail, Rock Cornish hens, capons, squab, and turkey.

Chicken

Chicken — perhaps the world's most popular meat – appears worldwide in many flavor combinations, often reflecting the traditional dishes of the country. Since chicken is so mild-flavored, it combines well with a myriad of ingredients — from strong-flavored vegetables, such as onions and peppers, to mild, sweet-flavored fruits, such as oranges and cherries, and even tart fruits, such as lemons and kumquats. Many low-fat preparations work well with poultry: barbecuing, baking, braising, boiling, broiling, grilling, poaching, roasting, spit-roasting, and stewing. Today, the choices of chicken are more than in years past: broiler-fryers, capons, free-range chickens, roasters, Rock Cornish hens, squabs (*poussins*), and stewing hens. Whole chickens are popular for boiling, roasting, and stewing; chicken parts are great for barbecuing, broiling, grilling, poaching, and sautéing. Boneless chicken breasts, often labeled fillets, are also perfect for barbecuing, grilling, and sautéing, as well as poaching, then tossing into salads.

Nutritionally, chicken is a very good source of protein: a 3-ounce portion of roasted or broiled chicken breast (without the skin) provides 52% of the Daily Value (DV) for protein. Chicken provides many vitamins and minerals, too — especially the B vitamin of niacin, which is needed for energy metabolism, normal growth, and the synthesis of fatty acids, DNA, and protein. A 3-ounce portion of boneless cooked chicken breast (without the skin) provides one-third (33%) of the DV for niacin.

Chicken livers are not only a rich source of vitamin A but also of many of the B vitamins, especially B_{12}, plus the minerals of iron and zinc. The iron in chicken is in a form that is easily absorbed by the body.

Here is a list of popular poultry available in most markets, listed in alphabetical order.

Broiler-fryers (2½ to 4½ pounds) are young chickens that are marketed when they are about 7 weeks old. They are tender, flavorful, and perfect for broiling, frying, and grilling.

Capons (8 to 10 pounds) are young neutered male chickens that are fed a fattening diet, then brought to market when they are 10 months old. They are fully breasted with more white meat than dark. Since the meat is juicy, sweet, and very flavorful, capons are the ideal birds to roast for a dinner party.

Roasters (5 to 7 pounds) yield more meat, pound for pound, than their smaller broiler-fryer cousins. As their name implies, they are best for roasting — in the oven and on the spit (rotisserie). Roasters are also delicious when poached, braised, and pot-roasted. Most are brought to market between 3 to 5 months old; plan on a 5-pound chicken (raw weight) to serve 5 to 6 people (from ¾ pound to 1 pound per person).

Rock Cornish hens (1½ to 2 pounds) are miniature hybrids of the Cornish and White Rock chickens. These little hens come to market when they are 4 to 6 weeks old. They are tender and juicy, but have little meat on their bones. Cook one hen for each person you are serving.

Stewing chickens (4 to 8 pounds) are also marketed as hens, stewing hens, or boiling fowl. These chickens range from

whole chicken

chicken parts   minced chicken

chicken sausages   duck parts

whole duck

10 to 18 months old, making them more flavorful, but also less tender, than a roasting chicken. They need long slow cooking in moist heat to tenderize them, so they are ideal for stewing or braising, or for making delicious homemade stock.

Chicken pieces can be found on and off the bone, with skin or skinless. Common chicken parts are breasts (whole and halves), skinless boneless breasts (often called fillets), thighs, drumsticks, quarters, and wings. The breast is the tenderest meat of the chicken with the least fat; thighs are the fattiest, thus the most moist.

Ground chicken is a great lower-fat alternative for ground beef in such recipes as hamburgers, meat loaves, and tacos. One 4-ounce ground chicken patty has 172 calories and 12 grams of fat, compared to a 4-ounce ground beef patty which has 300 calories (43% more) and 23 grams of fat (45% more).

Chicken products such as sausages can offer a lower-fat alternative to red meat products. They are usually less nutritious than a serving of chicken, because the meat often has been bulked up with other "filler" ingredients.

Duck

Duck has a similar protein content to chicken and turkey, but it is higher in fat. Most of the fat on a duck is found just below the skin. When preparing a duck for roasting, first cut away any visible fat, then prick the skin all over, to allow the fat to drain away. Roast, then discard the skin before serving.

Duck is rich in minerals, being a fair source of zinc and iron. Ounce for ounce, duck contains more than twice as much iron as chicken. It is a fair source of the B vitamins of niacin and riboflavin, and contains some potassium.

The ducks we buy today are usually of two species — the mallard and the muscovy. By far, one of the most popular ducks sold in the United States today is the white-feathered, broad-breasted Long Island ducks, a descendant of the Peking mallards. They are known for their dark, succulent, juicy meat.

Roasting ducks (3 to 5½ pounds) are young birds, no more than 16 weeks old. When buying a fresh duck, choose one with a plump broad breast and elastic skin. If the duck is frozen, be sure the package is tight and not broken.

Boneless duck breasts are quite popular; these breasts are perfect for pan-frying, grilling, barbecuing, and stir-frying.

versatile poultry

Goose

Like duck, goose is a waterfowl, and the rich dark meat of a goose contains much more fat than chicken and turkey. So it is important to cut away any visible fat, and prick the skin of the goose before roasting, in order for the fat to run out. Before serving, discard the skin.

Goose has a similar protein content to other poultry. A 3-ounce portion of roasted goose, without the skin, provides as much zinc and iron as a similar portion of cooked skinless duck. Goose also provides fair amounts of the B vitamins niacin, riboflavin, and B_6, as well as some copper. Small young geese, generally 6 to 8 months old, are called goslings; they normally weigh no more than 5 pounds. They have very tender meat that is less fatty than that of older geese. Female geese and male ganders (from 5 to 18 pounds) are older than goslings and have meat that is tougher and more fatty. There is much less meat on a goose than on a chicken or turkey, so when figuring out the size of bird to buy, allow about 1½ pounds of raw uncooked weight of goose per person.

Guinea fowl

As the legend goes, the small bird that is related to both the chicken and the partridge originated in Guinea, West Africa. Compared to chicken, the meat of the guinea fowl is dark, somewhat drier, and has a gamy, though pleasant, flavor. The smallest guinea hens, called guinea squabs, weigh about ¾ pound; the large guinea fowls, up to 4 pounds. Look for guinea fowl (either fresh or frozen) at specialty butcher shops. Prepare with moist heat — the more cooking liquid, the better.

Quail

Like guinea fowl and pigeon, quail is a bird that is now raised on game bird farms for the marketplace. They are very small, tender birds that should be roasted, fried, or broiled (watch carefully as they can overcook quickly). The meat is white and delicately flavored; often two birds are served per person. Nutritionally, they are similar to pheasant or partridge.

Squab

This young domesticated pigeon is raised on farms, has never flown, and is marketed when 4 weeks old, or less. Therefore, squabs are extremely tender. They weigh 1 pound or less, with rich dark sweet meat, and are fair sources of both iron and zinc. Frequently, squabs appear stuffed and roasted at some of the finest restaurants.

Squab chickens (*poussins*) have whiter meat, may be as old as 6 weeks, and weigh about 1½ pounds. These birds are best when broiled, grilled, or roasted.

Turkey

Though chicken has long been considered an everyday meat, turkey is traditionally reserved for such special occasions as Thanksgiving dinner. A large turkey, roasted to perfection, is the ideal bird for a celebration. It feeds a large gathering with plenty of leftovers for sandwiches and other meals.

Nutritionally, turkey is very similar to chicken, although it contains slightly more iron and zinc. Compared to the breast meat, the dark leg meat offers almost three times as much zinc and one and one-half times as much iron.

turkey breast steaks   quail   squab   guinea fowl   chicken

Sizing up the turkey

Judging how big a turkey to buy depends on how many people you want to serve, and the leftovers you want to enjoy over the next few days. Here is a turkey buying guide that allows for plenty of leftovers:

5- to 7-pound turkey serves	6 to 8 with leftovers
8- to 9-pound turkey serves	8 to 10 with leftovers
10- to 11-pound turkey serves	10 to 12 with leftovers
12- to 13-pound turkey serves	12 to 14 with leftovers
14- to 17-pound turkey serves	14 to 18 with leftovers
18- to 20-pound turkey serves	18 to 20 with leftovers

Whole turkeys vary greatly in weight. The male "tom" turkeys usually weigh in at 16 to 25 pounds; the smaller female hens, at 8 to 16 pounds. Relatively new to the marketplace are smaller fryer-roasters that weigh from 5 to 8 pounds and are marketed as the everyday turkey. Before shopping, check the chart *(above)*. Regardless of the season, whole turkeys, in all sizes, may be purchased either fresh or frozen. Some have a pop-up thermometer to help you know when they're done.

Turkey pieces (breasts, legs) Turkey breasts, both boneless and on the bone, as well as turkey legs and thighs on the bone, are easy to find in supermarkets and butcher shops. Today, they are marketed frozen year round, and are usually sold fresh most of the year. For single servings, look also for boneless turkey breast steaks, turkey *escalopes*, and turkey fillets.
Ground turkey makes a low-fat alternative to ground red beef. Use it for burgers and in meat sauces for dishes such as lasagna. A 4-ounce ground beef patty has 300 calories and 23 grams of fat; a ground turkey patty, only 170 calories and 9 grams of fat. That's 43% fewer calories and 60% less fat!
Turkey products such as sausages can be a good lower-fat choice, although many are breaded and deep-fried, which makes them high in fat. Turkey "rolls" and "roasts" can contain a lot of additives as well as water, so check the labels.

A buyer's guide to poultry

USDA Grade A chicken and poultry are the highest quality, and the only grade you are likely to find in the market today. Grade A means the poultry is plump and meaty, and free from defects, bruises, feathers, discolorations, and broken bones. When choosing poultry, look for fresh and plump birds without dry, discolored, or torn skin; avoid poultry with an unpleasant "off" odor. Be sure that the wrapping on a prepackaged bird is not torn and that the package is not leaking. If the bird is frozen, check that there is no freezer burn (brown or grayish-white patches on the skin). Be sure the "sell by" date on the package has not passed.

duck   goose   turkey

Glorious game

By definition, game birds are any wild birds that are suitable for food. In America, you can buy top-quality game birds in specialty meat markets, often frozen, cleaned, and ready to thaw and cook. Some mail-order companies sell game birds, which you can find in food-by-mail books and articles. Here are a few game birds to look for.

An ABC of game birds

Some game birds that once lived in the wild, such as duck, quail, and geese, are now farm-raised *(see Popular poultry, pages 12-15).* Pheasant and partridge are sometimes raised on game-bird farms and released for recreational hunting sports. Other birds, such as wild turkeys, remain truly wild, feeding on their traditional foliage rather than processed feed. Wild game birds get more exercise than their farm-raised cousins, so their meat tends to be darker in color with a stronger and more gamy flavor. The younger the bird, the more tender and leaner the meat.

Small young game birds, either farmed-raised or wild, are best when wrapped with bacon (known as barding) before roasting, grilling, or barbecuing. Large older birds, particularly wild game ones, tend to be tough and dry. They are best when cooked with a slow moist heat, such as in braising or pot-roasting, or when simmered slowly in soups and stews.

Hanging poultry and game birds

In the past, most meat and poultry, even fish, were "hung" to allow the naturally present enzymes and bacteria to break down and tenderize the meat. During this process, distinctive flavors developed.

Today, modern farming methods produce poultry and game birds that do not need to be hung. The muscles are not as developed, thus the birds are not as tough and do not need to be tenderized. However, on some game-bird farms, pheasant and wild duck are still hung in monitored conditions. Also, some producers of organic and free-range chickens and turkeys often hang poultry before they are "dressed" for the market.

Wild duck

The wild members of the duck family are much tougher, darker, and lower in fat than the younger farm-raised varieties, which are bred specifically for the market. Compared to the young farm-raised duck, the meat has a richer, more gamy flavor. Mallard is the most common and largest of the wild ducks; one duck provides only 2 to 3 servings. In comparison, the larger farm-raised Long Island ducks usually serve 6. Teal, the smallest wild duck, usually serves only 1. The shooting season for wild duck is September 1 to January 31.

Grouse

This small, ground-scratching game bird is hunted on moors in northern England and Scotland. The beginning of its shooting season is August 12, known as the "Glorious Twelfth," and ends on December 10. Grouse feed on heather, berries, and small insects; therefore, their dark red meat is strong and gamy in flavor. A young grouse weighs about 1¾ pounds and serves only 1 person. Grouse contains marginally more protein than other poultry, and is lower in fat.

Partridge

The partridge, which is a small game bird about the same size as grouse, is perhaps best known for its appearance in a pear tree in the traditional Christmas song. In fact, Christmas comes in the middle of the shooting season for partridge (September 1 to February 1). Partridge has pale meat with a delicate flavor — it is sometimes hung for 3 to 4 days before being dressed. One partridge makes 1 serving. Although not popular in the United States, partridge can be found, usually frozen, in some specialty butcher shops or by mail order.

Partridge has one of the highest meat protein contents, equaled only by venison, and a fat content of 7% in its meat.

Pheasant

Slightly larger than most other game birds, pheasant is quite tame; as a result, it is often raised on game-bird farms and used for hunting parties. The roasted meat of a pheasant has quite a gamy flavor. Modern tastes prefer pheasants that have not been hung. However, hanging older pheasants for several days before cooking them makes them more tender. A 3-pound pheasant (raw weight and on the bone) makes 2 to 3 servings when roasted, boned, and served.

Pheasant is an excellent source of protein. It is relatively high in fat for a game bird. Generally, the plump hen (female) birds contain more fat than the cocks (males). Pheasant is lower in iron than some other game birds, but is still a fair source for both iron and B vitamins.

Smaller game birds

Depending on where you live and the type of meat markets you have access to, other small game birds might be hunted in your area or might be available at your local butcher shop. Many arrive frozen. A few such wild birds are the dove, wild quail, thrush, and the two smallest game birds: snipe and woodcock. Because these birds are lean and small, they are best grilled, broiled, or roasted. For juicier meat, consider marinating the birds first. Avoid overcooking them.

Free-range versus mass-produced poultry

Free-range chickens are considered the elite of the poultry world. They frequently appear on menus in some of the finest restaurants across the country. In order to be labeled "free-range" or "free-roaming," the birds must be given access to the outside while they are being raised. Mass-produced birds are often raised in cages. In contrast, free-range birds are allowed to roam outside for their food. Some have inviting wooded areas; others, less comfortable open fields. As for their diet, these birds are often fed a special organic one (see below), according to many poultry breeders. Plus, as they roam, free-range chickens have the opportunity to eat a variety of natural foods. Most believe that these chickens have a better, more "chicken-y" flavor than their mass-produced cousins. Free-range birds are generally more expensive and usually sold in gourmet supermarkets and specialty meat markets.

What is organic poultry?

Organic chickens are understood to be birds that have been raised on land that has not been treated with chemical fertilizers or pesticides for at least three years. Their diet is believed to be free of all antibiotics, animal byproducts, hormones, and growth enhancers.They are fed entirely on chemical-free grains and are likely to also be free-range birds. They are usually sold whole.

How fast must I eat fast-food chicken?

When purchasing a cooked rotisserie or fast-food chicken, be sure it is hot and freshly cooked. Then eat and enjoy within 2 hours after buying it. After that, cut it up and refrigerate in a shallow covered dish, then eat within 2 days. Or wrap, freeze properly, and eat within 3 months.

partridge   grouse   pheasant   wild duck (mallard)

Handle with care

Thanks to the research, care, and production methods that the industry practices today, cooking and serving poultry at home is easier than ever—and safe—if you follow some important safety steps: Buy before the sell-by date on the package, refrigerate the birds quickly at home, and cook them within two days of buying them, or freeze.

Buying and handling poultry before cooking

By handling poultry properly and with care, you can cook and serve with confidence. Bacteria, which are naturally present in the air, water, soil, and on our bodies, may occasionally be found on raw poultry. Keep poultry safe by simply following these smart food-buying and handling procedures.

• Although not required by federal regulations, most poultry comes with a *sell-by date*. Do not buy if that date has passed.

• Buy poultry right before coming home. Pack it in a separate disposable plastic bag to keep juices away from other foods. Never leave raw poultry in a hot car. At home, refrigerate immediately (do not leave it at room temperature).

• Planning to cook the poultry within a few hours? Refrigerate it in its original package on a shallow dish to catch any juices. If storing the bird longer, unwrap (if it's a whole bird, remove the giblets from the body cavity first). Wash poultry with cold water, pat dry with paper towels, and place it in a shallow dish. Cover it with heavy-duty foil or plastic wrap, then store in the coldest part of your refrigerator (40°F or below).

• Use fresh poultry within 1 or 2 days after buying, or freeze.

• The pink liquid in the package is water (not blood) which the poultry absorbed during a chilling process. Discard it.

• When cutting up poultry, choose a surface of dense material, either sturdy plastic or a hardwood, such as maple. Afterwards, wash your hands and all utensils with hot soapy water.

• It's best to use one chopping board for raw poultry, meat and fish: a separate one for fruits, vegetables, and cooked foods.

• Always marinate poultry in a dish covered with plastic wrap. Let marinate in the refrigerator, never at room temperature.

• If you plan to use the leftover marinade for basting or as a dipping sauce, first bring it to a full boil (212°F) for 1 minute. This temperature kills any bacteria that might be present.

Freezing the bird

• If you cannot use *fresh* poultry within 2 days, freeze it.

• When buying poultry that has been frozen, then thawed, be sure to use it without freezing it again. *Tip:* If parts of a package of poultry feels hard and firm, while other parts of the same package feel soft and fresh, the poultry has probably been frozen. Buy only if you plan to cook it within 2 days.

• Before freezing, first rinse poultry with cold water and pat dry with paper towels. Freeze poultry at 0°F or below.

• Discard the original packages the poultry came in. Place in *freezer-weight* plastic bags or wrap airtight in heavy-duty foil.

• If freezing a whole bird, remove the giblets and rinse out the cavities first. Then wrap the bird in freezer paper and seal.

• If freezing pieces or cubes of poultry, lay them on a tray, then freeze until firm. Place in self-sealing freezer bags, seal, and return to freezer. For the best quality, use within 6 months.

▲ Place poultry in a shallow dish and cover securely before placing it in the coldest part of the refrigerator (40°F or below).

- Never freeze a stuffed bird, either cooked or uncooked. Remove the stuffing first and freeze it separately.

Thawing whole birds in the refrigerator

Weight of frozen bird (in pounds)	Thawing time
3 to 5	18 hours to 1 day
7 to 10	1½ to 2 days
12 to 15	2 to 2½ days
16 to 20	2½ to 3 days
22 to 25	3 to 3½ days

Thawing the bird

- Thaw poultry in the refrigerator — not at room temperature. General rule of thumb: Allow about 5 hours of thawing time in the refrigerator for every pound of frozen poultry, that is 24 hours (1 day) for every 5 pounds. Check out the chart above.
- To quick-thaw raw or cooked chicken, use the microwave and follow the manufacturer's directions. Cook immediately!
- Or, to thaw in cold water, place poultry in a water-tight plastic bag, then immerse it in cold water. Allow about 30 minutes of thawing time for every pound of frozen poultry.
- Thaw poultry *completely*, then use it immediately or refrigerate until time to cook; avoid holding it overnight.

When cooking poultry

- When grilling poultry outdoors, keep it in the refrigerator until it's time to put it on the grill.
- Place the *cooked* poultry on a clean plate.
- When grilling or broiling pieces of chicken (breast, legs, and thighs), place the dark meat on the grill about 10 minutes before the breasts (white meat takes less time to cook).
- When roasting a whole bird or a turkey breast, loosely cover the breast with a tent of foil during the last hour of cooking.
- For the juiciest birds, baste frequently during roasting.

- Never partially roast any poultry one day and finish cooking it the next (bacteria might grow under such conditions).
- Before carving, let the bird rest for 10 to 20 minutes (no longer!) to allow the juices to firm up.
- Serve poultry quickly after cooking it, within a half-hour, then refrigerate leftovers immediately at the end of the meal.

Stuffing the bird

When stuffing the bird, follow these steps the USDA suggests:
- Mix the stuffing right before it goes into the bird.
- Stuff the bird loosely — don't pack it in! Allow about ¾ cup of stuffing per pound. Truss the bird, then immediately place the bird into a preheated 325°F oven.
- Spoon any extra stuffing that does not fit in the bird into a shallow buttered baking dish. Cover with foil and refrigerate it. Bake the stuffing, still covered, in the same oven (325° or 350°F) with the bird during the last 30 minutes.
- Before removing the bird from the oven, make sure the stuffing reaches a temperature of 165°F and the turkey reaches a temperature of 180°F (use a thermometer!). Remember: A pop-up indicator tests only the turkey, not the stuffing.

Trussing

Tuck the wing tips under the bird's back and loosely tie the ends of the legs. A tighter trussing may keep the bird in a neat compact shape, but it also may prevent the leg meat from cooking through as rapidly as the less-fatty breast meat.

▲ After stuffing the neck cavity, you don't need to truss the bird. Instead, just secure the flap of skin in place with the wing tips.

Is it done yet?

- Cook chicken well done, not medium or rare.
- Here's a perfect way to check if the bird is ready to eat: Pierce the thickest part of the bird with a fork (if you're roasting a whole bird, pierce the thigh, not the breast, for doneness). A chicken, turkey, or goose is done when the juices run clear, no longer pink. In contrast, the juices of a raw duck or most game birds will be a little pink.
- Insert an instant-read thermometer into the thigh (do not touch the bone) or the thickest part of the meat being roasted. The bird is ready to eat when the thermometer reads:
    - 180° to 185°F for a whole chicken or turkey (unstuffed)
    - 180° to 185°F for a whole stuffed chicken or turkey and 165°F for the stuffing
    - 170°F for chicken or turkey breast or parts on the bone
    - 160°F for boneless chicken or turkey parts
    - 185° to 190°F for a whole duck (stuffed or unstuffed)
    - 190° for a whole goose (stuffed or unstuffed)

▼ An instant-read thermometer is the most accurate way to tell when the bird and its stuffing are thoroughly cooked and ready to eat.

▲ To freeze cooked poultry in gravy, slice the meat off of the bones, then layer it in a freezer container. Cover meat completely with gravy.

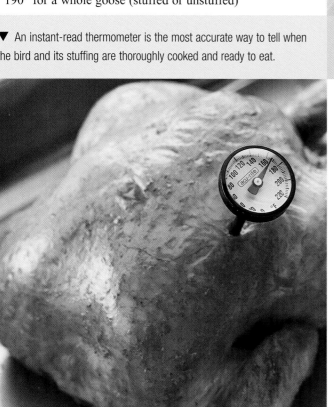

If not eating immediately

As soon as poultry is cooked, scoop out the stuffing into a serving bowl, then let the bird set for 10-20 minutes before slicing. Serve the stuffing and the bird quickly after slicing.

- Have leftovers? Refrigerate them immediately after the meal is over (within an hour after bringing the bird out of the oven).
- If the bird was stuffed, refrigerate leftover stuffing in a covered container, away from the meat (use within 3 days).
- Cut leftover meat off the bone immediately after serving. Wrap in plastic wrap or foil; refrigerate (use within 3 days).
- Reheat cooked poultry only once. To reheat meat in gravy or a sauce, bring mixture slowly to a boil over medium heat and cook for 5 minutes. Or reheat in the microwave, stirring during cooking, until the food is piping hot throughout.
- Freeze cooked stuffing and cooked meat (off the bones) separately in a plastic freezer bag. Use within 3 months.
- If you wish, freeze cooked meat in gravy, covering it completely; leave an inch of space at the top of the container.

A world of flavors

As the recipes in this book prove, poultry and game birds are wonderfully versatile. You can grill them, braise them, roast them, broil them, stew them, and simmer them into soups. As you cook, experiment with the almost endless range of flavorings that work well. Take some tips from cooks in different countries. Spice chicken with saffron for a Spanish paella; add hot Indian spices for a curry; grill with a jerk sauce for a Jamaican barbecue. Team up turkey as they do in Mexico with a chili and chocolate mole sauce; stuff it the old-fashioned American way with a fresh-herb and bread stuffing and serve with cranberry sauce. Flavor chicken with cumin and fresh mint and stuff into pitas, as they do in Greece; season duck with five spices and stir-fry, as they do in China; drizzle a chicken salad with a sesame-soy dressing as in Japan.

To get you started, here are some popular flavorings that go well with the mild flavors of poultry:

pungent flavorings such as onions, garlic, fresh gingerroot, shallots, chives, and cilantro;

delicate herbs such as tarragon, basil, parsley (both curly and flat-leaf), coriander, chervil, dill weed, mint, and savory;

robust herbs such as thyme, rosemary, lemon grass, bay leaf, marjoram, oregano, sage, and saffron;

warm spices such as juniper berries, allspice, curry powder, star anise, cumin, caraway seeds, cardamom, celery seeds, cinnamon, fennel, mace, nutmeg, paprika, and sesame seeds;

hot spices such as chilies (fresh, dried, and ground), peppercorns (black, white, green, and pink), mustard (seeds and ground), ground ginger, and turmeric;

fruit and nuts such as citrus (oranges, lemons, and limes), mangoes, cranberries, cashews, and chestnuts.

pungent flavorings

delicate herbs

robust herbs

warm spices

hot spices

fruit and nuts

Back to basics

Lower-fat cooking methods are perfect for poultry and game birds. Baking, barbecuing, boiling, braising, broiling, grilling, poaching, roasting, steaming, stewing, stir-frying — they are all low-fat ways of cooking that work well. With the leftover bones and bits of meat, make a well-flavored stock or soup.

Taking off the fat

Most of the fat in many birds is in the skin. Discard the skin, either before or after cooking, and you reduce the total fat content of the dish at the same time. When roasting, grilling, or barbecuing, leave the skin on the bird during cooking to hold in the juices, them remove the skin before serving. Or, discard the skin before cooking and let the bird stand in a flavor-filled marinade for at least an hour or overnight. The marinade adds flavor to the bird and also helps keep it moist during cooking.

Marinades

A marinade is a seasoned liquid that flavors, tenderizes, and adds moisture — all at the same time. Most marinades contain an acid (such as lemon juice, vinegar, or wine) for tenderizing, and herbs and spices for flavoring. For young tender poultry, 1 hour of marinating in the refrigerator is fine; for an older, tougher game bird, let it marinate overnight in the refrigerator.

a yogurt marinade adds flavor

Tips for lower-fat cooking

- Roasting a bird? Season the bird first by gently lifting up the skin and spreading reduced-fat cream cheese and fresh thyme leaves over the breast. Or, tuck in slivers of onions, bits of turkey bacon, and thin peeled apple slices; or try reduced-fat sour cream and fresh rosemary.

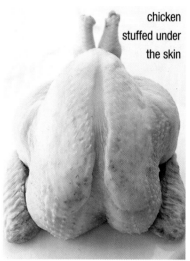

chicken stuffed under the skin

- Game birds are traditionally barded, that is wrapped with slices of bacon or pork fat, to keep the naturally lean breast meat moist. Try lower fat options of turkey bacon or thin slices of prosciutto. They work well on skinless chicken breasts, too (leave the bone in but remove the skin before wrapping with the bacon).
- When roasting a chicken, fit the roasting pan with a rack and place the bird on top. This keeps the fatty drippings away from the bird as it roasts. Afterwards, remove the bird and rack, and use a gravy strainer to skim off the fat from the drippings. Then, whisk the meat juices into a gravy or sauce.
- Roast the bird upside-down for the first half of the roasting time. The fat from the turkey drips down into the breast, not into the pan. The juices keep the breast moist (no extra butter-basting is needed). Brush with an herbed wine, if you wish.
- Baste with a low-fat marinade, such as apple cider, lemonade, cranberry juice, marsala, or white wine.
- Stuff the bird with a flavor mix of vegetables (onions, celery, and carrots) or lemon halves and sprigs of marjoram. Discard stuffing after roasting (the flavors bake into the bird).

Homemade chicken stock

Ask any good chef. You will likely hear that one secret of success in the kitchen is to start with a good homemade stock. A perfectly seasoned chicken stock is the start of many dishes — from soups to stews, sauces, sautés, gravies, and casseroles. Unlike some stocks, this rich stock begins with pieces of dark meat of chicken or turkey on the bone, such as legs and thighs, instead of a chicken or turkey carcass. But either work well.

Makes 3½ quarts of stock

4½ quarts cold water (18 cups)

5 pounds chicken or turkey pieces on the bone (legs and thighs)

2 large yellow onions, quartered

3 large carrots, scrubbed and cut into 1-inch chunks

3 ribs celery with leaves, cut into 1-inch chunks

1 medium-size white turnip, peeled and cut into 1-inch cubes

5 large cloves garlic, peeled

1 large bunch fresh parsley (about 15 sprigs)

8 sprigs fresh thyme

2 large dried bay leaves

24 black peppercorns

1 teaspoon salt

Preparation time: 15 minutes
Cooking time: 2½ hours

1 In a 10- or 12-quart saucepot, bring the water and chicken pieces to a full boil over high heat, skimming off any foam that rises to the surface. Stir in the onions, carrots, celery, turnip, and garlic. Then stir in the rest of the ingredients.

2 Return the mixture to a full boil. Reduce the heat to medium-low. Simmer the mixture gently (do not cover!) for 2½ hours. Stir occasionally to keep the ingredients mixed.

3 Carefully strain the stock through a large strainer or sieve into a large heatproof bowl, discarding the meat, bones, vegetables, herbs, bay leaves, and peppercorns.

4 If using the stock while still hot, skim off any visible fat from the surface with a spoon. Preferably, let the stock cool to room temperature, then cover and refrigerate until it is cold. Using a spoon, scrape away all of the fat that has risen to the surface. Use refrigerated stock within 3 days, or freeze the stock and use with 3 months.

Another idea

● Roasted chicken stock: At the beginning of step 1, preheat the oven to 450°F. In a large roasting pan, spread out the chicken pieces; roast uncovered for 15 minutes. Stir in the onions, carrots, celery, turnip, and garlic and roast 15 minutes more. Transfer the meat and vegetables to the stockpot of water and bring to a full boil. Add the rest of the ingredients, then proceed with step 2.

Stuffings for the bird

Pack poultry stuffings with plenty of bread, vegetables, fruits, and seasonings. You will have a stuffing that's not only low in fat, but also high in carbohydrates, fiber, and flavor. Stuff into the bird, or shape and bake small stuffing balls alongside.

Old-fashioned apple-bread stuffing

Makes 8 cups stuffing (plenty for a 5-pound bird)

½ cup pitted prunes or apricots

¼ cup port, dry red wine, or fresh orange juice

2 large red baking apples, such as Rome Beauty or Cortland

3 large ribs celery

1 extra-large yellow onion

2 tablespoons unsalted butter

8 cups day-old bread cubes (16 slices)

1 cup coarsely chopped walnuts, toasted

¼ cup *each* fresh chopped parsley and sage

1 teaspoon poultry seasoning

1 teaspoon freshly ground black pepper

1 cup chicken stock, preferably homemade
  or low-sodium chicken broth

1 large egg, beaten

Preparation time: 30 minutes

Cooking time: 25 minutes (or inside cavity of bird)

1 Using scissors, snip the prunes or apricots into small ½-inch pieces. Place the fruit in a small saucepan, add the port, and bring to a simmer over medium heat. The fruit will become plump and absorb the liquid. Transfer to a large bowl.

2 Peel and core the apples and cut into bite-size pieces. Coarsely chop the celery; peel and chop the onion. In a large skillet, melt the butter over medium-high heat. Add the apples, celery, and onion and sauté for 5 minutes or until crisp-tender. Transfer to the bowl with the prunes or apricots.

3 Add the bread cubes and mix well, then stir in the walnuts, parsley, sage, poultry seasoning, and pepper. Gently stir in the chicken stock and egg just until the ingredients are moistened (do not over-mix as this may make the stuffing tough).

4 Stuff into the neck and body cavities of a chicken or turkey. Shape any leftover stuffing into 2-inch balls. Refrigerate the balls, then bake on a buttered baking sheet in the same oven with the bird (at 325°F or 350°F) during the last 25 minutes of roasting. Stuffing is done at 165°F; the turkey, at 180°F.

Another idea

• Golden bread stuffing: Substitute 6 cups dry corn bread stuffing mix for the bread cubes (step 3). Increase the chicken stock to 2 cups; heat to boiling before adding to the apple and stuffing mixture (step 3).

Sausage and chestnut stuffing

Makes 8 cups stuffing (plenty for a 5-pound bird)

1 pound premium chicken sausages

1 extra-large yellow onion, peeled and coarsely chopped

6 cups dry herb-seasoned stuffing (cubes)

1 cup chopped roasted chestnuts or 1 cup chopped pecans, toasted

2 tablespoons chopped fresh sage

2 tablespoons chopped fresh marjoram

¼ teaspoon ground nutmeg

1 teaspoon freshly ground black pepper

2½ cups chicken stock, preferably homemade (see page 23),
   or low-sodium chicken broth

1 large egg

Preparation time: 30 minutes
Cooking time: 25 to 30 minutes (or inside cavity of bird)

1 Remove the sausage meat from the casings. Spray a large nonstick skillet with cooking spray and heat over medium-high heat. Add sausage and onion and sauté for 5 minutes or until the sausage is brown and the onion is tender. Transfer to a large bowl.

2 Add the dry stuffing and mix well, then stir in the chestnuts or pecans, the sage, marjoram, nutmeg, and pepper.

3 In a small saucepan, bring the chicken stock to a boil over high heat. Whisk the egg in a large measuring cup, then pour into the hot stock and whisk to blend. Add to the stuffing mixture and stir gently just until the ingredients are moistened (do not overmix as this may make the stuffing tough).

4 Stuff into the neck and body cavities of a chicken or turkey with the stuffing *(see page 19)*. Or, place in a buttered 8-inch-square baking dish, cover with foil, and bake at 325°F for 30 minutes, or at 350°F for 25 minutes, or until the temperature of the stuffing reaches 165°F and the bird reaches 180°F.

Another idea

• Simple sausage and sage stuffing: Omit chestnuts (step 2). Increase the sage to 3 tablespoons; omit the marjoram (step 2).

Beginnings

Soups, satays, and pâté

THINK POULTRY — right from the beginning. Start
homemade soups with chunks of chicken or turkey and
plenty of fresh vegetables. Simmer them slowly into
a creamy chicken corn chowder, an Asian soup flavored
with lemon grass, or a hearty turkey soup. Make a light,
elegant mousse from chicken livers, onions, and a splash
of brandy. Begin a party with chicken rolled up in flaky
phyllo or with a delectable duck pâté that's layered with
fresh green beans and baked in a terrine. Some summery
evening, kick off supper with
skewers of chicken and vegetables,
hot off the grill. They are all great
beginnings for dishes high on
flavor and nutrition, too.

Turkey, chestnut, and barley soup

One of the best parts of roasting a turkey is making a big pot of soup from the rest of the bird. If you're not roasting a bird, use canned chicken broth instead of the homemade stock. Add wintery vegetables and chestnuts.

Makes 8 servings

Homemade Turkey Stock

1 turkey carcass (from at least a 12-pound bird) or 5 pounds turkey parts, on bone

1 large yellow onion, peeled and quartered

2 large ribs celery, coarsely chopped

10 sprigs *each* fresh parsley and thyme

1 large bay leaf

12 black peppercorns

1 teaspoon salt

Turkey Soup

2 pounds cooked turkey breast (boneless)

3 large carrots, peeled and chopped (2 cups)

4 large turnips, peeled and chopped (2 cups)

4 large ribs celery, chopped (2 cups)

6 ounces pearl onions, peeled (2 cups)

⅓ cup pearl barley

8 ounces Brussels sprouts, halved or chopped

½ cup coarsely chopped chestnuts

¼ cup chopped fresh parsley

Preparation time: 45 minutes

Cooking time: about 2 hours

Each serving (1½ cups) provides

calories 200, total fat 2g, saturated fat 0g, cholesterol 47mg, sodium 361mg, total carbohydrate 24g, dietary fiber 5g, protein 22g

✓✓✓	A, C
✓✓	niacin, B_6
✓	B_1, B_2, folate, iron, magnesium, potassium, zinc, copper, fiber

1 First, make the stock. Break up the turkey carcass, discarding any skin, and place in an 8-quart stockpot. Add enough cold water to cover (about 12 cups) and bring to a boil over high heat; skim off any foam with a slotted spoon. Add the remaining ingredients for the stock and return to a full boil.

2 Lower the heat and simmer the stock gently, uncovered, for 1½ hours. Strain and discard the bones and vegetables (you need 9 cups of stock). Skim off any fat and return the stock to the stockpot.

3 To make the soup, return the stock to a boil. Remove the skin from the turkey breast and cut the turkey into bite-size pieces (you need 6 cups). Add the turkey to the stockpot, along with the carrots, turnips, celery, onions, and barley. Simmer the soup, uncovered, for 30 minutes or until the barley is tender.

4 Add the sprouts and chestnuts and simmer 5 minutes more or just until the sprouts are crisp-tender. Sprinkle with the parsley and serve steaming hot.

More ideas

• In-a-hurry turkey soup: Substitute 9 cups of canned low-sodium chicken broth for the homemade turkey stock (steps 1 and 2). Pour the stock into the stockpot and bring to a boil over high heat. Proceed by adding and cooking the vegetables (steps 3 and 4).

• Vegetable garden turkey soup: Substitute ½ cup of uncooked white rice for the barley (step 3). Omit the sprouts and chestnuts (step 4); add 2 cups of fresh or frozen green peas and 1 cup of chopped tomatoes. Simmer 10 minutes more if using fresh peas (only 5 minutes more for frozen peas).

• Turkey noodle soup: Omit the barley, sprouts, and chestnuts. Decrease the cooking time from 30 minutes to 15 minutes (step 3). Add 1 cup uncooked angel hair pasta (capelli d'angelo) and 1 cup of chopped red bell pepper (step 4). Return to a boil and cook 3 to 5 minutes or until pasta is tender. Sprinkle with the parsley, then top with ½ cup chopped dry roasted peanuts.

Healthy tips

• Barley is believed to be the world's oldest cultivated grain. It is low in fat and rich in carbohydrates. Like many other cereals, it is also a good source of B vitamins, which are essential for a healthy nervous system and helping the body transform food into energy. Pearl barley has had the outer husk and the bran removed, plus it has been steamed and polished.

• Compared to almonds, walnuts, and pecans, chestnuts are high in carbohydrates and low in fat and calories. Plus, ⅓ cup of chestnuts gives a fair source of vitamin C.

beginnings

Chicken and fresh corn chowder

Here's a chowder that tastes rich and creamy, but is made with low-fat milk instead of cream. If it's fresh corn season, cut off the kernels. Any other time, use frozen corn kernels. Stir them up with chicken and potatoes and crumble crisp bacon on top. Supper is served — with chunks of crusty bread and a crisp vegetable salad.

Makes 4 servings

4 large ears yellow corn on the cob

1 tablespoon sunflower oil

1 extra-large onion, finely chopped (2 cups)

2 large potatoes, peeled and cut into ¾-inch dice (2 cups)

2½ cups chicken stock, preferably homemade (see page 23)

2 cups low-fat milk (2% milkfat)

1 pound cooked chicken breasts (boneless and skinless), cut into bite-size pieces

2 teaspoons chopped fresh tarragon or ¾ teaspoon dried

½ teaspoon freshly ground black pepper

To decorate

4 slices turkey bacon

Fresh tarragon leaves

Preparation time: 30 minutes

Cooking time: 25 minutes

Each serving (1½ cups) provides

calories 473, total fat 14g, saturated fat 4g, cholesterol 90mg, sodium 518mg, total carbohydrate 52g, dietary fiber 6g, protein 40g

✓✓✓	niacin
✓✓	B₁, B₂, B₆, C, potassium
✓	A, B₁₂, folate, D, calcium, iron, magnesium, zinc, copper, fiber

1 Remove the green husks and all the silk from the corn. Stand each cob on the wide stem end on a chopping board, at an angle. Cut the corn kernels off the cob with a serrated knife (you need 2 cups of kernels). Set aside.

2 In a large saucepan, heat the oil over medium-high heat. Add the onion and sauté for 5 minutes or until tender, but not brown. Stir in the potatoes and corn kernels and cook 5 minutes more, stirring frequently. Pour in the chicken stock and bring to a boil. Lower the heat to medium-low and simmer gently for 5 minutes or until the potatoes are tender, but not breaking apart.

3 Stir in the milk, one-third of the chicken, the chopped tarragon and pepper. Cook, stirring gently, 3 minutes more or until hot.

4 Pour one-third of the mixture into a food processor or blender and blend to a coarse texture, not to a purée. Return to the pan. Stir in the rest of the chicken and heat the chowder until hot.

5 In a medium-size skillet, cook the bacon over medium-high heat until golden brown and crisp. Drain on paper towels, then crumble. Ladle the chowder into 4 bowls. Sprinkle each bowl with one-fourth of the bacon and a few tarragon leaves. Serve steaming hot.

Healthy tips

● Milk is an excellent source of dietary calcium, necessary for building healthy bones and teeth. It also contains many important nutrients, including protein (casein), carbohydrates (lactose), and the water-soluble B vitamin of riboflavin. Most low-fat milk products are fortified with the fat-soluble vitamins A and D.

● Sweet corn contains some protein, but it is an incomplete protein because it lacks two essential amino acids (tryptophan and lysine). When eaten with beans or other legumes, it provides a complete protein.

● Contrary to common belief, one medium boiled potato (about 5 ounces) is low in fat. It is a good source of vitamins B₆ and C, and a fair source of the minerals potassium and copper.

More ideas

• Chicken and mushroom chowder: After preparing the corn (step 1), vertically slice 8 ounces trimmed white mushrooms (you need 3 cups). In a large skillet, sauté the mushrooms in 2 tablespoons unsalted butter over medium-high heat for 5 minutes; add 2 tablespoons of Madeira wine and continue cooking until most of the liquid evaporates. Add mushrooms with the potatoes and corn (step 2). Tip: Mushrooms are low in fat and have no cholesterol.

• Wintertime chowder: When fresh corn is not in the market, substitute 10 ounces frozen corn kernels for the corn on the cob. Omit step 1. After sautéing potatoes, add frozen kernels (no need to thaw) with the chicken stock (step 2).

• Baked croutons: Instead of bacon, garnish the soup with croutons. Preheat the oven to 350°F. Trim the crusts off of 4 slices of cracked wheat bread, whole-wheat bread, or thick country white bread. In a cup, mix 2 tablespoons of olive oil with 1 teaspoon of garlic salt and

½ teaspoon of freshly ground black pepper; brush on both sides of the bread. Cut the bread into ½-inch cubes and spread the croutons in a single layer on a baking sheet. Bake croutons for 10 minutes or until golden, turning once. Sprinkle the baked croutons with a mixture of 2 tablespoons of chopped fresh parsley and 2 tablespoons of grated Parmesan cheese. Return the croutons to the oven and bake for 5 minutes more or until golden brown and crisp, tossing one more time during baking.

beginnings

31

Chicken with lemon grass

One taste of this lovely hearty soup, and you'll think you've just taken a trip to Southeast Asia. Chicken contributes protein; zucchini and string beans add nutrients; sprigs of lemon grass give a rich citrus touch. Bruising (partially crushing) the lemon grass with the back of a knife helps release its flavor during cooking.

Makes 4 servings

3½ cups cold water

1 teaspoon salt

½ teaspoon freshly ground black pepper

1 small fresh chili pepper

1 large garlic clove, peeled and halved

½-inch piece fresh gingerroot, peeled

2 stalks lemon grass, bruised and cut in half, plus extra sprigs for decorating

2 pounds chicken breasts, on the bone

3 tablespoons minced shallots

10 ounces string beans or French haricots verts, trimmed and cut in half (2½ cups)

1 large zucchini, cut lengthwise into thin 3-inch matchsticks (2 cups)

⅓ cup canned cream of coconut

2 teaspoons finely grated lime zest

3 tablespoons fresh lime juice

2 tablespoons chopped fresh coriander

Preparation time: 30 minutes

Infusing time: 30 minutes

Cooking time: 28 minutes

Each serving (1½ cups) provides

calories 310, total fat 15g, saturated fat 8g, cholesterol 78mg, sodium 620mg, total carbohydrate 14g, dietary fiber 3g, protein 32g

✓✓✓	C
✓✓	niacin
✓	A, B_1, B_2, B_6, iron, magnesium, potassium, zinc, copper, fiber

1 In a large saucepan, pour in the water and add the salt and pepper. Split open the chili pepper lengthwise, but leave whole. Spear the pepper with the garlic and gingerroot on a wooden bamboo skewer (this makes them easy to remove later) and drop into the saucepan with the lemon grass stalks. Bring to a boil over high heat; boil for 1 minute. Remove from the heat, cover, and let stand to infuse for 30 minutes.

2 Return the liquid to a boil, then reduce the heat to low. Add the chicken and shallots: poach, uncovered, for 8 minutes. Add the string beans and zucchini and continue cooking for 5 minutes more or until the juices of the chicken run clear when a breast is pierced with a fork.

3 Using a slotted spoon, transfer the chicken, string beans, and zucchini to a bowl. Drizzle on a little of the poaching liquid to keep them moist, cover tightly, and keep warm.

4 Return the liquid in the saucepan to a boil and stir in the cream of coconut until dissolved. Continue boiling the liquid for 5 minutes or until the liquid has reduced by one-third.

5 Shred the chicken meat, discarding skin and bones. Return the chicken and vegetables to the soup. Heat for 3 minutes more or until hot. Remove from the heat and discard the lemon grass and skewer of chili, garlic, and gingerroot. Stir in the grated lime zest and juice. Sprinkle with coriander; top with a few sprigs of lemon grass.

More ideas

● Chinese chicken-noodle soup: Cook 1½ cups of Chinese egg noodles according to package instructions, then drain them well. Stir into the soup with the chicken and vegetables (step 5).

● Springtime chicken soup: Substitute 2 cups of fresh asparagus tips for the string beans (step 2).

● Choosing chili peppers: Generally, the smaller the pepper, the hotter it will be. If it's too hot for your taste, discard the seeds and membranes. Some fresh chilis (from the hottest to milder) are red Scotch bonnet, bright red serrano, greenish-red Fresno, green jalapeño, green Anaheim, and dark green poblano.

Healthy tips

● French beans and zucchini add some nutrients, such as vitamins and fiber, to this hearty, delicious chowder.

● Breast of chicken is one of the best sources of the B vitamin niacin. It is needed for the metabolism of energy and for keeping the skin, nervous system, and digestive system healthy.

beginnings

Duck terrine and citrus-plum salsa

Traditionally, a terrine is a coarsely ground, highly seasoned meat, fish, or poultry baked without a crust in a pork-fat-lined container (a terrine). For a lower-fat version, grind trimmed duck breasts with leeks, orange zest, and just a little duck fat, then layer with fresh green beans. Line the mold or pan with paper, instead of extra fat.

Makes 8 servings

Duck terrine

1 tablespoon extra virgin olive oil
1 pound leeks or white onions, thinly sliced
2 large garlic cloves, minced
3 large oranges
6 fresh sage leaves
1 cup green beans (haricots verts), trimmed
1 pound boneless duck breasts
1 tablespoon fresh thyme leaves
2 tablespoons brandy
½ teaspoon *each* salt and black pepper

Citrus-plum salsa

1 pound reddish-purple ripe plums
½ cup chopped fresh orange sections
½ cup finely chopped red onion
1 tablespoon orange liqueur or orange juice
½ teaspoon *each* salt and black pepper

Preparation time: 45 minutes
Baking time: 1½ hours
Cooling and chilling time: at least 13 hours

Each serving provides

calories 215, total fat 4g, saturated fat 1g,
cholesterol 81mg, sodium 340mg, total
carbohydrate 26g, dietary fiber 4g, protein 18g

✓✓✓	C
✓✓	niacin, iron
✓	B₆, folate, potassium, fiber

1 In a large saucepan, heat the oil over medium-high heat. Add the leeks and garlic, then reduce the heat to medium-low, cover, and cook for 20 minutes or until soft. Let cool.

2 Meanwhile, preheat the oven to 350°F. Line the bottom and sides of a 1-pound earthenware terrine or 8½"x 4½"x 2½" loaf pan with wax or parchment paper. Grate the zest from the oranges and set aside. Peel the oranges, then cut one of the oranges into slices, ¼ inch thick, and section the other 2 oranges (for the salsa and for decorating). Attractively arrange the sage leaves and orange slices on the bottom of the tin. Set aside.

3 Half-fill a small saucepan with water and bring to a boil over high heat. Add the green beans and cook for 2 minutes, or until bright green and crisp-tender. Rinse under cold water. Dry on paper towels and set aside.

4 Remove the skin and fat from the duck breasts, reserving ½ cup of the fat, and discarding the rest, along with all of the skin. Coarsely chop the meat and add to the bowl of the food processor along with the ½ cup of fat, 2 tablespoons of the orange zest, the thyme, brandy, salt, and pepper. Pulse until ground to a paste. Add the cooked leeks; pulse once more (do not purée).

5 Carefully spoon half of the duck mixture on top of the oranges and sage leaves in the terrine. Using a small metal spatula, carefully pack down the mixture and smooth out the surface. Arrange the green beans lengthwise in a single layer. Spoon on the rest of the duck mixture and smooth the surface.

6 Cover the loaf tin with foil. Place it in a baking pan at least double its size and pour in enough boiling water to come halfway up the sides of the terrine. Bake for 1½ hours or until the juices run clear when the center of the terrine is pierced with a knife.

7 Transfer the terrine to a wire rack. Cut out a piece of cardboard to cover the top of the terrine and weight it down. Let the terrine stand at room temperature for 1 hour to cool, then refrigerate for at least 12 hours.

8 Now, make the salsa. Peel and pit the plums. Finely chop them and place in a medium-size bowl. Mix in all of the remaining salsa ingredients. Cover and chill at least 15 minutes.

9 To serve, loosen the sides of the terrine with a knife and invert it onto a platter. Gently peel off the paper, being careful to keep the design. Let the terrine come to room temperature and decorate with the rest of the orange sections. Slice and serve with the salsa.

More ideas

• Savory chicken terrine: Substitute 1 pound of boneless skinless chicken thighs for the duck breast (step 4). Use 4 slices of chopped turkey bacon instead of duck fat; add 1 tablespoon of fresh marjoram leaves with the thyme (step 4).

• Three-fruit salsa (great with the chicken terrine): Omit the citrus-plum salsa (step 8). Instead, coarsely chop 2 cups of pink grapefruit sections and 1 cup of orange sections and place in a medium-size bowl. Stir in ¼ cup of minced green onions, 1 minced fresh green chili (discard the membranes and seeds), 2 tablespoons of finely chopped fresh mint leaves, and ½ teaspoon *each* of salt and black pepper. Let stand for 15 minutes; drain well.

• Hot and spicy salsa: Make the salsa, omitting the orange liqueur. Remove the seeds and membrane from 1 small fresh red chili pepper, finely chop, and stir into the salsa. Add 2 tablespoons of Marsala wine. This salsa is a delicious complement to the duck terrine.

beginnings

Chicken liver mousse

Instead of frying chicken livers, poach them in a savory stock with onions and vegetables. Then purée them and season with a sprinkle of pepper, some white wine vinegar, and a splash of brandy. You'll have a chicken liver mousse with the creaminess and flavor of a traditional liver mousse but one that is less dense and rich.

Makes 1 cup

12 ounces chicken livers, well trimmed

2 large yellow onions, finely chopped (2 cups)

1 large garlic clove, minced

8 sprigs of fresh parsley, about 5 inches long

8 sprigs of fresh thyme, about 5 inches long

1 large bay leaf

4 cups chicken stock or canned chicken broth

2 tablespoons reduced-fat cream cheese
(Neufchâtel)

1 tablespoon brandy or Calvados, or to taste

2 teaspoons white wine vinegar

1 teaspoon salt

½ teaspoon freshly ground black pepper

1 tablespoon pink or green peppercorns in
brine, drained and dried on paper towels,
or capers

¼ cup finely chopped fresh parsley

Triangles of white country bread, toasted

Preparation time: 30 minutes

Cooking time: 15 minutes

Chilling time: at least 4 hours or overnight

2 tablespoons liver mousse provide

calories 110, total fat 4g, saturated fat 1g, cholesterol 271mg, sodium 478mg, total carbohydrate 6g, dietary fiber 1g, protein 13g

✓✓✓	A, B$_{12}$, folate
✓✓	B$_2$
✓	niacin, B$_6$, C, iron, zinc

1 In a large saucepan, place the chicken livers, onion, and garlic. Place the parsley, thyme, and bay leaf in the center of a square of cheesecloth, then tie into a bouquet garni; add to the saucepan. Pour over the stock, adding a little water if necessary to cover all of the ingredients. Slowly bring to a boil over medium-high heat, skimming away the foam. Lower the heat to medium-low and simmer gently for 8 minutes or until the livers are cooked but still slightly pink in the center.

2 Drain and discard the bouquet garni. Transfer the livers, onions, and garlic to a food processor. Add the cream cheese, brandy, vinegar, salt, and ground pepper; process until smooth. Transfer to a bowl and stir in the peppercorns. If you do not have a food processor, mash the livers, onions, and garlic into a coarse paste with a fork, then stir in the rest of the ingredients (except the parsley and toasted bread).

3 Spoon the mousse into a serving bowl, or individual ramekins, and smooth the top with a knife. Sprinkle with the parsley. Cover with plastic wrap and chill for at least 4 hours, but preferably overnight.

4 Before serving, allow the mousse to return to room temperature. Serve with the toast triangles.

More ideas

● Country pâté: Add ¾ cup of canned cannellini beans, rinsed and dried on paper towels, to the food processor with the chicken livers, onion, and garlic (step 2). Add 2 teaspoons of finely chopped fresh sage leaves. Serve on slices of white peasant bread or sourdough bread and decorate with sliced gherkins.

● Citrus-chicken mousse: Use 1 tablespoon of grated orange zest and ¼ cup of fresh orange juice instead of the brandy (step 2).

● Chicken liver on pumpernickel: For a delicious sandwich, spread a generous amount of the mousse on a slice of pumpernickel bread. Top with thin slices of red onion and unpeeled red apple. Cover with a second slice of bread.

● Flavor with fresh herbs: Try adding different seasonings, such as 2 tablespoons of chopped fresh chives, tarragon, or mint leaves to the mousse (step 2).

Healthy tips

● Chicken livers are a good source of iron. Each serving of this mousse provides a fair amount of the Daily Value for iron.

● Many traditional recipes for chicken liver mousse and pâté seal the surface with a layer of melted or clarified butter for storage. In this recipe, chopped fresh herbs add extra flavor. Then the mousse is sealed with plastic wrap instead of a layer of butter.

beginnings

37

Chicken satays

In Indonesia, satays (also satés) are a popular snack. Small bite-size pieces of poultry, meat, or seafood are first marinated in a spicy mixture, then grilled on wooden skewers and served with a peanut sauce. Here, cubes of chicken are flavored with spicy ginger and skewered with colorful crunchy vegetables and wedges of fresh lime.

Makes 8 appetizer servings

Marinade

¾-inch piece fresh gingerroot, peeled and
   finely chopped
2 tablespoons low-sodium soy sauce
2 tablespoons fresh lime juice
1 tablespoon peanut oil

Satays

1 pound boneless skinless chicken breasts
2 large yellow bell peppers
1 large zucchini (12 ounces)
1 large lime, cut into 8 wedges
8 large cherry tomatoes

Peanut sauce

2 teaspoons peanut oil
1 small yellow onion, finely chopped (½ cup)
1 large garlic clove, minced
1 teaspoon green Thai curry paste or
   ¾ teaspoon curry powder
⅓ cup unsalted peanuts, finely chopped
⅔ cup water
¼ cup canned cream of coconut
1 tablespoon low-sodium soy sauce
½ teaspoon sugar

To decorate

Sprigs of fresh coriander

Preparation time: 30 minutes
Marinating time: 30 minutes
Cooking time: 23 minutes

1 First, make the marinade. Mix the gingerroot, soy sauce, lime juice, and oil in a bowl. Cut the chicken into 1¼-inch cubes, add to the marinade, and toss to coat. Cover with plastic wrap and let marinate in the refrigerator for 30 minutes, turning twice.

2 Soak 8 wooden skewers in cold water for at least 30 minutes. Meanwhile, remove the stems and seeds from the bell peppers, then cut into 1¼-inch squares. Cut the zucchini in half lengthwise (do not peel); place each half on a cutting board, cut-side down, and cut crosswise into half circles, ¾ inch thick. Cut the lime lengthwise into 8 wedges and wash the cherry tomatoes. Set aside.

3 Now, make the peanut sauce. In a small saucepan, heat the oil, add the onion, garlic, and curry paste; sauté over medium-high heat for 3 minutes. Add the peanuts and continue sautéing 5 minutes more or until both the nuts and onion are lightly browned. Add the water, cream of coconut, soy sauce, and sugar and bring to a boil. Reduce the heat to medium-low and simmer gently, uncovered, for 5 minutes or until thickened, stirring occasionally. Transfer the sauce to a food processor and purée into a smooth thick cream. Return to the saucepan; keep hot.

4 Preheat the grill or broiler to high. Thread the chicken, vegetables, and lime wedges alternately onto the soaked skewers. In a small saucepan, bring the marinade to a boil. Grill or broil 6" from the heat, basting often with the marinade for 10 minutes, turning, until golden brown and the juices of the chicken run clear when it is pierced with a fork. Decorate the satays with the coriander; serve with the sauce.

Healthy tip

● Most of the fat in peanuts is the unsaturated kind. Recent studies suggest that diets containing a daily intake of peanuts, peanut butter, or peanut oil may help to lower total cholesterol, particularly the harmful LDL cholesterol, helping to protect against coronary heart disease.

Each satay provides
calories 187, total fat 10g, saturated fat 4g, cholesterol 34mg, sodium 272mg, total carbohydrate 10g, dietary fiber 2g, protein 16g

✓✓✓	C
✓✓	niacin
✓	B$_6$, magnesium, potassium

More ideas

- Chicken and fruit satays: Substitute 2 cups of fresh pineapple chunks (1 inch cubes), 2 cups banana slices (½ inch thick), and 1 large green bell pepper for the yellow peppers, zucchini, and lime (step 2).
- Summer satays: Substitute 2 cups of yellow summer squash semicircles (¾ inch thick), 1 large red onion (cut into 8 wedges), and 1 large red bell pepper for the yellow peppers, zucchini, and lime (step 2).
- Vegetable garden satays: Instead of the yellow peppers, zucchini, and lime, use 1½ cups of parboiled new potatoes (cut in half before cooking), 1 cup of parboiled peeled baby carrots, and 1 large red bell pepper.
- Main-dish kebabs: Cook 2 cups long-grain white rice (or a combination of long-grain white and wild rice) according to package directions; toss with ½ cup of sliced green onions. For each serving, arrange 2 satays on a bed of the rice. To serve, drizzle the peanut sauce generously over the rice and the kebabs. This main-dish variation makes 4 servings.

beginnings

39

Chicken and vegetable phyllo rolls

For low-fat great-tasting appetizers, start with thin sheets of pastry made from a flour and water mixture, called phyllo (the Greek word for leaf). Cut the pastry sheets into strips and fill them with a minced chicken filling mixed with fresh vegetables, herbs, and a little smoked ham. Serve with spicy piquant cranberry mustard.

Makes 8 servings

2 large carrots, peeled and cut into
  1 x ⅛ x ⅛ -inch julienne strips (1 cup)
4 ounces savoy cabbage with curly dark
  green leaves, shredded (2 cups)
⅓ cup slivered green onions (about 3)
8 ounces ground uncooked chicken breast
  (1½ cups)
½ cup lean cooked smoked ham, minced
½ cup finely chopped yellow onion
2 tablespoons dry plain bread crumbs
2 teaspoons chopped fresh sage leaves
2 teaspoons chopped fresh thyme leaves
1 teaspoon freshly ground black pepper
¼ teaspoon salt
8 large sheets phyllo pastry (18x14 inches)
¼ cup (½ stick) unsalted butter, melted
2 teaspoons sesame seeds

Cranberry mustard

⅓ cup canned jellied cranberry sauce
2 tablespoons red wine vinegar
1 tablespoon extra virgin olive oil
1 teaspoon Dijon mustard

To serve

2 cups mesclun salad greens

Preparation time: 45 minutes
Baking time: 30 minutes

1 First, make the filling. Half-fill a medium-size saucepan with water and bring to a boil over high heat. Add the carrots, cabbage, and green onions, then blanch for 1 minute. Transfer to a colander and rinse immediately with cold running water. Pat the vegetables dry with paper towels and place in a large bowl. Mix in the chicken, ham, yellow onion, bread crumbs, sage, thyme, pepper, and salt; set aside.

2 Preheat the oven to 375°F and set out a nonstick baking sheet. Now, shape the pastries. On a flat surface, cut the 8 phyllo sheets in half lengthwise, making 16 pieces. Trim each into a thin strip, 15 inches by 6 inches and quickly cover, first with plastic wrap then with a damp towel (phyllo dries in a couple of minutes if left uncovered). Work fast!

3 For each phyllo roll, use 2 pastry strips. Brush one pastry strip lightly with butter, then top with a second strip. Brush it lightly with butter, too. Place an eighth of the filling across one end of this pastry strip. Roll up the filling inside the pastry, folding in the long sides as you go and making a closed parcel, about 5 inches long and 2 inches in diameter. Place the parcels on a baking sheet, seam-side down, and brush with a little more butter. Repeat, making a total of 8 rolls.

4 Using a serrated knife, make 3 shallow diagonal slashes across the top of each parcel. Brush with the rest of the butter; sprinkle with sesame seeds. Bake 30 minutes or until golden.

5 Meanwhile, shake all of the cranberry mustard ingredients in a screw-top jar until well blended. Drizzle a little cranberry mustard around the edge of each of 8 small plates, mound some salad greens in the center, and place a phyllo roll on top.

Healthy tips

• Unlike butter pastry, phyllo is low in fat and calories. One sheet (18 x 14 inches, about 1 ounce) contains 2 grams of fat and just 85 calories. The same weight of butter pastry contains 6 grams of fat and 110 calories.
• By mixing plenty of vegetables with the chicken, you reduce the amount of fat in each phyllo roll and add extra vitamins and dietary fiber at the same time.

1 roll + 1 tablespoon mustard provides
calories 225, total fat 11g, saturated fat 5g, cholesterol 37mg, sodium 321mg, total carbohydrate 21g, dietary fiber 2g, protein 11g

✓✓✓	A
✓	B₁, niacin, B₆, C

beginnings

40

More ideas

- Greek spinach and chicken phyllo pockets: Substitute 2 cups slivered fresh spinach leaves for the cabbage (step 1). Omit the ham, bread crumbs, and sage. To the vegetables add the chicken, onion, thyme, pepper, and salt, plus ½ cup cooked white rice and 3 tablespoons fresh lemon juice (end of step 1). Cut the 8 phyllo sheets into 16 six-inch squares. For each phyllo parcel, brush one square with butter, cover with a second square and brush with a little more butter. Place one-eighth of the filling in a triangular shape, slightly off-center, near one corner. Fold the pastry over the filling to make a triangular parcel, matching up the opposite corner and sealing the sides (step 3). Sprinkle with 2 teaspoons poppy seeds instead of the sesame seeds. Bake for 30 minutes as directed (step 4) and serve on the salad leaves. Omit the cranberry mustard (step 5).

- Oriental egg rolls: Substitute 1½ cups fresh bean sprouts for the cabbage (step 1). Substitute 1 cup chopped, cooked, and deveined peeled fresh shrimp for the ham (end of step 1). Roll and bake as directed (steps 3 and 4). Substitute ½ cup bottled plum sauce for the cranberry mustard (step 5).

Sensational Salads

Plenty of substance, goodness, and flavor

Toss POULTRY INTO THE SALAD BOWL with ripe fruits, fresh vegetables, shells of pasta, grains of rice, and plenty of fresh herbs. Drizzle with dressings that complement, then serve with confidence, knowing you're dishing up big helpings of goodness as well as flavor. Oven-fry strips of sesame chicken the healthier way and serve on crunchy cabbage and crisp greens. Arrange slices of warm marinated duck on baby greens and drizzle with a citrus vinaigrette. Toss pieces of smoked chicken with melon and fresh pineapple. Or stir-fry chicken with turkey bacon, spoon on top of avocados and tomatoes, and splash with a hot honey-mustard vinaigrette.

Warm sesame chicken salad

Take strips of chicken and shake them up in a mixture of sesame seeds, bread crumbs, cornflakes, and a dash of chili powder. Bake them, instead of frying them, until crunchy and crispy. Serve on a fresh vegetable salad.

Makes 4 servings

1 pound boneless skinless chicken breasts

½ cup dried unseasoned bread crumbs

½ cup cornflakes crumbs

1 tablespoon sesame seeds, plus extra
   to decorate

1 teaspoon hot chili powder, or to taste

2 large eggs

Salad

½ large head white cabbage, shredded

1 head frisée (curly yellow-white leaves)

2 heads chicory (dark green curly leaves)

Herb dressing

¼ cup extra virgin olive oil

3 tablespoons white wine vinegar

2 tablespoons chopped fresh tarragon leaves

2 tablespoons chopped fresh oregano leaves

2 teaspoons golden honey

½ teaspoon *each* salt and ground pepper

Preparation time: 30 minutes

Cooking time: 10 minutes

Each serving provides

calories 445, total fat 22g, saturated fat 4g,
cholesterol 176mg, sodium 584mg, total
carbohydrate 30g, dietary fiber 7g, protein 35g

✓✓✓	A, niacin, folate, C
✓✓	B₂, B₆, calcium, magnesium, potassium, copper, fiber
✓	B₁, iron, zinc

1 Preheat the oven to 400°F. Set out 2 nonstick baking sheets. Cut the chicken breasts into 3- or 4-inch strips, 1 inch wide.

2 In a paper or plastic bag, shake the bread crumbs, cornflake crumbs, 1 tablespoon sesame seeds, and the chili powder until well mixed. In a shallow dish, whisk the eggs until frothy.

3 Dip the chicken strips, one at a time, into the beaten eggs, then drop into the bag. When 5 or 6 pieces of chicken are in the bag, shake them until they are coated evenly with the sesame seed mixture. Spread out the coated strips on the baking sheets (without touching). Repeat until all pieces are coated. Bake the chicken strips for 10 to 12 minutes, turning them over once.

4 Meanwhile, make the salad. In a large salad bowl, place the shredded cabbage. Pull the frisée and chicory leaves apart and tear any large ones into 2 same-size pieces. Add to the salad bowl.

5 Now, make the dressing. In a small screw-top jar, shake together all of the dressing ingredients. Drizzle over the salad and toss well. Divide the salad among 4 luncheon salad plates and pile the cooked chicken pieces on top. Sprinkle with a few more sesame seeds and serve the salad while the chicken is still warm.

More ideas

• Orange chicken: Omit dried bread crumbs and sesame seeds. For the coating, increase the cornflake crumbs to 1 cup; add 2 tablespoons of grated orange zest (step 2). Add 1 cup of fresh orange sections (step 4).

• Chinese sesame chicken salad: Make the crumb mixture by substituting 2 teaspoons of five-spice powder and ¼ teaspoon of salt for the sesame seeds and chili powder (step 2). To the eggs, whisk in 2 tablespoons of low-sodium soy sauce, 2 tablespoons of sweet sherry, and 1 tablespoon of poppy seeds (step 2). Coat and bake the chicken strips as directed. Replace the salad with 1 large head of shredded bok choy (discard any hard white core) and toss with 1 cup of fresh bean sprouts and ¾ cup of sliced green onions (step 4). To the dressing add 2 tablespoons *each* of chopped fresh coriander and chopped parsley (step 5).

Healthy tips

• Cabbage and chicory are low in fat and good sources of fiber.

• Both cabbage and chicory provide a good amount of vitamin C and folate. One of the B vitamins, folate is essential for a healthy pregnancy. Women need a good amount of folate before conceiving, and in the early stage of their pregnancy, in order to prevent spina bifida, a neurological defect of the spinal column.

sensational salads

Stir-fried chicken and avocado salad with hot balsamic dressing

Quickly stir-fry chicken with bits of turkey bacon. Season with a hot dressing that is sweetened with honey, sparked with vinegar, and spiced up with a little mustard. Serve on top of a fresh green salad tossed with rich avocado slices, fresh cherry tomatoes, and slivers of red onion. Luncheon, or even supper, is served!

Makes 6 servings

Tomato and avocado salad

2 heads Boston lettuce, separated into leaves
1 bunch watercress
2 large ripe avocados
3 tablespoons fresh lemon juice
1 pint cherry tomatoes (2 cups)
1 small red onion

Stir-fried chicken

1 pound boneless skinless chicken breasts
2 tablespoons extra virgin olive oil
2 large garlic cloves, cut into slivers
2 tablespoons golden honey
1 tablespoon whole grain Dijon mustard
1 tablespoon balsamic vinegar
6 strips smoked turkey bacon, diced

Preparation time: 20 minutes
Cooking time: 7 minutes

Each serving provides
calories 348, **total fat 22g, saturated fat 4g, cholesterol 55mg, sodium 336mg, total carbohydrate 18g, dietary fiber 5g, protein 23g**

✓✓✓	C
✓✓	niacin, B_6, folate, potassium
✓	A, B_1, B_2, iron, magnesium, copper, fiber

1 First, prepare the salad. In a large salad bowl, place the lettuce leaves. Trim the tips of the watercress and toss with the lettuce (you will have about 9 cups of greens). Peel the avocados, cut in half, and discard the seeds. Slice the avocados lengthwise, ½ inch thick, and toss with the lemon juice. Cut the tomatoes in half and the onion into thin slivers. Scatter the avocados, tomatoes, and red onion on top of the salad and refrigerate.

2 Now, stir-fry the chicken. Cut the chicken into 3- to 4-inch strips, 1 inch wide. In a large skillet or wok, heat the oil over medium-high heat. Add the chicken strips and garlic and stir-fry for 3 minutes or until the chicken turns opaque.

3 Add the honey, mustard, and vinegar and stir to mix well. Add the diced turkey bacon and stir-fry for 3 minutes more or until the bacon is cooked and the chicken is tender and moist (do not overcook).

4 Spoon the stir-fried chicken strips, bacon, and any liquid remaining in the skillet on top of the salad. Serve with wedges of warm crusty bread.

More ideas

● Cobb salad with stir-fried chicken: Substitute 1 cup of sliced green onions for the red onion (step 1). Before serving, sprinkle the salad with ½ cup of crumbled Roquefort cheese (step 3).

● Chicken, spinach, and orange salad: Substitute 5 cups of fresh baby spinach leaves and 2 cups of orange sections for the Boston lettuce and tomatoes (step 1).

● Turkey-artichoke salad: Substitute one 10-ounce jar of well-drained marinated artichokes for the avocados (step 1). In the salad, omit the 3 tablespoons of fresh lemon juice, but add them to the skillet instead with the honey, vinegar, and mustard (step 3). Use 1 pound turkey steaks (boneless and skinless) for the chicken breasts (step 2).

Healthy tips

● Ounce per ounce, turkey bacon contains one-third less fat than pork bacon and one-third fewer calories.

● Monounsaturated fat, which is most of the fat in avocados, does not tend to elevate blood cholesterol levels. Avocados are a fair source of potassium, the mineral that helps maintain the balance of fluids in the body.

sensational salads

Pasta and chicken salad with basil

Here's a pasta salad that's high in carbohydrates and low in fat, thanks to the vinaigrette dressing that's made with two-thirds vinegar and lemon juice and only one-third olive oil. Be sure to toss the cooked pasta and snow peas with the dressing so they soak up the tangy taste. Fresh basil leaves add even more flavor.

Makes 6 servings

White wine vinaigrette dressing

1 cup dry white wine vinegar

6 tablespoons extra virgin olive oil

½ cup fresh lemon juice

1 tablespoon grated lemon zest

½ teaspoon freshly ground black pepper

Pasta and chicken salad

1 teaspoon salt

½ teaspoon freshly ground black pepper

4 cups uncooked seashell pasta

4 ounces snow peas, trimmed (1½ cups)

1½ pounds boneless skinless chicken breasts

5 large ripe plum tomatoes

1 tablespoon extra virgin olive oil

3 large cloves garlic, peeled and thinly sliced

½ cup pitted black olives

2 cups fresh basil leaves

Preparation time: 15 minutes
Cooking time: 15 minutes

Each serving provides
calories 590, total fat 23g, saturated fat 3g, cholesterol 69mg, sodium 497mg, total carbohydrate 64g, dietary fiber 2g, protein 37g

✓✓✓	B$_1$, niacin, C
✓✓	B$_2$, B$_6$, iron,
✓	magnesium, potassium, zinc, copper

1 First, make the dressing. In a small jar with a screw top, pour in all of the ingredients for the dressing. Shake to mix well and set aside.

2 Now, make the salad. Half-fill a saucepot with water, add ½ teaspoon of the salt, and bring to a boil over high heat. Add the pasta and return to a boil. Cook, uncovered, according to package directions or until the pasta is al dente. Drop in the snow peas and cook 2 minutes more. Transfer to a colander, rinse with cold water, and let stand until well drained.

3 Transfer the pasta and snow peas to a large salad bowl. Sprinkle with the remaining ½ teaspoon of salt and the pepper. Shake the dressing again and drizzle over the pasta mixture. Toss until well coated and let stand to soak up the flavors.

4 Cut the chicken into bite-size pieces. Cut each of the tomatoes lengthwise into 6 wedges. In a large skillet, heat the oil over high heat. Add the chicken and garlic and stir-fry for 5 minutes or until the chicken is lightly browned and the juices run clear when a piece is pierced with a fork. Toss the chicken with the pasta mixture. Scatter the tomatoes and olives over the top. Sprinkle with the basil leaves.

Healthy tips

• The vitamin C provided by the freshly squeezed lemon juice and the tomatoes helps the body absorb iron from the chicken.

• Pasta is low in fat and is an excellent source of carbohydrates. It also contains valuable vitamins, in particular the water-soluble B vitamins, which we need to eat daily, since our body does not store them.

More ideas

• Chicken and rice salad: Omit the seashell pasta (step 2). Instead, cook 2 cups of white rice with ½ teaspoon of salt, according to package directions, until all of the water is absorbed. In a separate saucepan, cook the snow peas in boiling water for 2 minutes or just until crisp-tender; drain well. Transfer the rice and the snow peas to a large salad bowl (step 3). Season the mixture with the remaining ½ teaspoon of the salt and the pepper. Continue making the salad as directed (step 4).

• Rest-of-the-chicken salad: Add 1 large minced garlic clove to the dressing (step 1). Substitute 3 cups of bite-size cooked chicken breasts (boneless and skinless) for the uncooked chicken breasts (step 4). Stir-fry for only 3 minutes, not 5, or just until heated through. Toss with the pasta and snow peas and top with the tomatoes, olives, and basil.

sensational salads

Grilled quail salad with Madeira

Today, most quail are farm-raised and sold either fresh or frozen in speciality meat markets. They often come flattened out, on wire skewers, ready for grilling. The meat is white and delicately flavored. Here, Madeira, a Portuguese wine, and juniper berries enrich the flavors. This recipe works well for chicken breasts or thighs.

Makes 4 servings

8 quail (about 5 ounces each), dressed and
   giblets removed

Madeira marinade

¾ cup Madeira wine
2 large garlic cloves, minced
1 large sprig of fresh thyme (5 inches)
1 large bay leaf
4 juniper berries, lightly crushed (optional)

Vegetable salad

3 cups fresh bean sprouts
8 ounces shiitake mushrooms, sliced (3 cups)
2 cups chopped fennel (about 8 ounces)
2 tablespoons fresh thyme leaves

Red wine vinaigrette

⅓ cup Madeira wine
2 tablespoons Dijon mustard
2 tablespoons walnut oil or olive oil
2 tablespoons red wine vinegar
½ teaspoon sugar
½ teaspoon *each* salt and black pepper

To decorate

2 cups mesclun salad greens
2 green onions, coarsely chopped (½ cup)
8 sprigs of fresh thyme

Preparation time: 30 minutes
Marinating time: at least 1 hour or overnight
Cooking time: 12 minutes

1 Often, quail come prepared for cooking with their backbones removed, then flattened out, and skewered. If not, prepare the quail. Using a boning knife or poultry shears, cut along both sides of the backbone of each quail and lift it out (avoid cutting through the skin). Place the quail on a flat surface, skin-side up, and press down firmly with the palm of your hand to flatten out the birds. Weave 2 parallel skewers (at least 12 inches) through each bird to hold it flat. Spread out the birds in a single layer, breast-side down, in a large shallow dish.

2 Now, make the marinade. In a large measuring cup, whisk all of the ingredients for the Madeira marinade; pour over the quail. Cover with plastic wrap and marinate in the refrigerator for at least 1 hour or overnight, turning the birds at least one time.

3 Now make the salad and vinaigrette. In a large salad bowl, toss all of the ingredients for the vegetable salad; set aside. In a small screw-top jar, place all of the ingredients for the vinaigrette and shake until blended. Set aside.

4 Now grill the quail. Preheat the grill or broiler to high. Lift the quail out of the marinade; discard the bay leaf. In a small saucepan, bring the marinade to a boil over high heat. Place the birds on the grill rack, about 6 inches from the heat. Cook the birds for a total of 12 minutes or until the juices of the quail run clear when a thigh is pierced with a fork. Baste often with the remaining marinade, turning the quail once.

5 To serve, shake the vinaigrette again, drizzle over the vegetable salad, and toss until well coated. Divide the mesclun salad greens among 4 serving plates and spoon one-fourth of the vegetables on top. Remove the skewers from the quail and place 2 quail on each bed of vegetables. Decorate each plate with one-fourth of the green onions and 2 thyme sprigs.

Each serving provides

calories 432, total fat 21g, saturated fat 4g, cholesterol 83mg, sodium 562mg, total carbohydrate 22g, dietary fiber 3g, protein 27g

✓✓✓	niacin, C, copper
✓✓	B₁, B₂, B₆, folate, iron
✓	A, E, magnesium, potassium, fiber

sensational salads

50

More ideas

• Grilled chicken breast with Burgundy: Substitute 4 large chicken breast halves on the bone, with skin (about 8 ounces each), for the quail (step 1). Leave the chicken breasts on the bone and do not skewer them. For the marinade, substitute ¾ cup of white Burgundy wine for the Madeira and 1 tablespoon of chopped fresh rosemary leaves for the juniper berries (step 2). Increase the grilling time to 12 to 15 minutes or until the juices of the chicken run clear when a breast is pierced with a fork. To serve, remove the skin, if you wish, and slice the meat 1 inch thick. Arrange on top of the salad for serving (step 5.

• Carrot, corn, and zucchini salad: Omit this sprout vegetable salad. Substitute with a tossed salad: 2 cups of peeled grated carrots, 2 cups of thin matchsticks of zucchini, 2 cups of sweet onion rings (such as Vidalia), and 2 cups of blanched yellow corn kernels (step 3). Toss with the red wine vinaigrette (step 5).

Healthy tips

• Bean sprouts are a good source of folate, the B vitamin that the body needs to make red blood cells. Folate also synthesizes certain amino acids, which the body uses to make protein. Sprouts also provide a good source of vitamin C.

• By serving vegetables raw, as in this salad, you preserve many of the vitamins that would be destroyed by cooking.

51

Smoked chicken and fruit salad

For a chicken salad with a terrific flavor, start with tender smoked chicken. Toss it with both white and wild rice, then add fresh honeydew balls and chunks of juicy pineapple. For the dressing, just squeeze some fresh oranges, instead of using an oil-based dressing that adds calories. This salad is best the day it's made.

Makes 6 servings

4 cups water

½ teaspoon salt

1 cup long-grain white rice

1 cup wild rice

1 pound cooked smoked chicken breasts (boneless and skinless)

1 large honeydew melon

1 large pineapple

1 tablespoon grated orange zest

¾ cup fresh orange juice

½ teaspoon freshly ground black pepper

To serve

6 large Boston lettuce leaves

¼ cup finely chopped fresh tarragon or parsley

Preparation time: 20 minutes

Cooking time: about 30 minutes

Each serving (1½ cups) provides

calories 416, total fat 2g, saturated fat 0g, cholesterol 63mg, sodium 981mg, total carbohydrate 79g, dietary fiber 4g, protein 24g

✓✓✓	niacin, C
✓✓	B$_1$, B$_6$, magnesium, potassium
✓	B$_2$, folate, iron, zinc, copper, fiber

1 In a large saucepan, bring the water and salt to a boil. Add the long-grain and the wild rice and cook according to package directions, until the rice is tender. Transfer to a colander, rinse with cold water, and drain well.

2 While the rice is cooking, mix the salad in a large bowl. First, cut the chicken into bite-size pieces. Cut the melon in half, discard the seeds, and scoop out the fruit with a melon baller. Peel and core the pineapple, then cut into bite-size wedges. Gently fold in the drained rice. Stir in the orange zest and juice; sprinkle with the pepper.

3 Line a large serving plate with the lettuce leaves. Spoon on the salad and sprinkle with the tarragon. Serve at room temperature or chilled.

Healthy tips

● Low in fat and high in carbohydrates, rice is an ideal food for a healthy diet. Because it is a complex carbohydrate, it provides a slow, steady supply of glucose for energy.

● This salad is rich in vitamins – B vitamins in the rice and vitamin C in the melon, pineapple, and orange juice.

● The vitamin C in this salad helps the body absorb the iron from the chicken.

More ideas

● Smoked turkey salad with dried cherries: Substitute 1 pound of a smoked turkey breast, cut into bite-size pieces, for the smoked chicken (step 2). Soak 1 cup of dried cherries in hot water for 5 minutes and drain well. Add to the salad with the melon and pineapple (step 2).

● Smoked chicken and apple fruit salad: Use 2 large unpeeled red Delicious apples instead of the melon. Core and cut into ¾-inch chunks (do not peel). Toss them with 2 tablespoons of fresh lemon juice and add to the chicken, pineapple, and rice mixture (step 2). Instead of the tarragon, sprinkle the salad with ½ cup of toasted chopped walnuts (step 3).

● Smoked chicken, green grape, and melon salad: Substitute 1 large cantaloupe for the honeydew. Add 1 cup of green grapes, cut in half, with the melon and pineapple (step 2). Instead of the tarragon, sprinkle the salad with ½ cup toasted slivered almonds (step 3).

● Smoked turkey and minted fruit salad: Prepare the salad using 1 pound of a smoked turkey breast, cut into bite-size pieces, instead of the smoked chicken (step 2). Substitute ¼ cup slivered fresh mint leaves for the fresh tarragon (step 3).

Warm duck salad with bulghur

For a delicious warm supper salad, try this one featuring lean duck breasts marinated in a spicy, lemony orange vinaigrette sparked with fresh basil. Cook the duck breasts the way you like them and arrange on a mound of bulghur with sweet kumquats scattered around. Then, sprinkle chopped fresh tomatoes and cucumber over all.

Makes 4 servings

Citrus vinaigrette

1 tablespoon grated orange zest

2 cups fresh orange juice

½ cup slivered fresh basil leaves

½ cup fresh lemon juice

3 large garlic cloves, minced

3 tablespoons extra virgin olive oil

3 tablespoons balsamic vinegar

1½ tablespoons mild chili powder

1½ teaspoons ground cumin

½ teaspoon salt

½ teaspoon freshly ground black pepper

Duck salad

4 boneless duck breasts (6 ounces each)

16 kumquats

1½ cups water

½ cup fresh orange juice

½ cup sugar

1 cup bulghur

¾ cup sliced green onions

8 cups mesclun salad greens

1 large beefsteak tomato, diced (2 cups)

½ large unpeeled cucumber (1 cup)

Preparation time: 45 minutes

Cooking time: 30 minutes

1 First, make the vinaigrette. In a large measuring cup, whisk all of the ingredients for the vinaigrette.

2 Now, prepare the salad. Remove the skin and fat from the duck breasts, then place in a single layer in a large shallow dish. Drizzle with ½ cup of the vinaigrette, cover with plastic wrap, and place in the refrigerator to marinate.

3 To prepare the kumquats, cut a small X in the side of each one (do not cut all the way through). Place the kumquats in a medium-size saucepan with the water, orange juice, and sugar. Bring to a boil over high heat, reduce the heat to medium, and simmer, uncovered, for 15 minutes or until the kumquats are tender. Set aside to cool in the liquid.

4 Cook the bulghur according to the package directions. Transfer to a colander, drain well, and place in a large bowl. Toss with the green onions and ½ cup of the vinaigrette.

5 Spray a large nonstick skillet with nonstick cooking spray and heat over medium-high heat. Transfer the duck breasts from the marinade to the skillet (discard the marinade). Cook the duck, turning once, for 8 minutes or until they are done the way you like them. Transfer to a carving board and slice very thinly against the grain.

6 Line a large serving platter (or 4 individual plates) with the salad greens. Mound the bulghur mixture in the center and arrange the duck slices in a circle, placing the slices against the bulghur. Scatter the kumquats around. Whisk ¼ cup of the kumquat cooking syrup into the remaining vinaigrette and drizzle over the salad. Sprinkle with the cucumber and tomato, and serve.

Healthy tips

- Oranges and kumquats are both excellent sources of vitamin C. This vitamin helps to build teeth and bones and promotes the healing of wounds. It also works to keep the immune system healthy and helps the body absorb iron from the food we eat.
- Bulghur wheat is a good source of fiber and magnesium, and also provides some copper and folate.

Each serving provides

calories 582, **total fat** 17g, **saturated fat** 3g, **cholesterol** 38mg, **sodium** 356mg, **total carbohydrate** 96g, **dietary fiber** 18g, **protein** 19g

✓✓✓	folate, C, fiber
✓✓	A, B$_1$, B$_2$, niacin, B$_6$, iron, magnesium, potassium, copper
✓	calcium, zinc

sensational salads

More ideas

● Warm duck salad with wild rice: Prepare one 6-ounce package of long-grain and wild rice mix according to package directions; toss with ⅓ cup of toasted pecans. Omit the bulghur and substitute the wild rice mixture (step 4).

● Grilled duck salad: Instead of cooking the duck in a skillet (step 5), preheat the grill or broiler to high and brush the rack with a little olive oil. Measure out ¼ cup of bottled Chinese duck sauce. Grill the duck breasts 6" from the heat for about 10 minutes, turning once, or until

they are the way you like them. Brush frequently with the duck sauce during cooking.

● Warm duck salad with tangerines: Omit the kumquats and their preparation (step 3). Instead, toss 3 cups of fresh tangerine sections with the bulghur mixture (step 4).

Turkey salad with red cabbage

Any time of year, but especially around the holidays and in midwinter, this crisp salad is delightful. Toss bites of turkey with red cabbage, carrots, celery, and sweet golden raisins, then add toasted pecans and caraway seeds. Make the flavors sparkle with a drizzle of cranberry vinaigrette made from walnut oil and wine vinegar.

Makes 6 servings

Cranberry vinaigrette

⅓ cup canned cranberry jelly

3 tablespoons red wine vinegar

2 tablespoons extra virgin olive oil

2 tablespoons walnut oil

½ teaspoon salt

½ teaspoon freshly ground black pepper

Turkey-vegetable salad

½ cup coarsely chopped pecans

½ teaspoon caraway seeds

1½ pounds cold roasted turkey breast
(boneless and skinless)

1 small red cabbage (1 pound), shredded
(4 cups)

2 large carrots, peeled and shredded (1 cup)

2 ribs celery, sliced (1 cup)

½ cup golden raisins

Preparation time: 30 minutes

Cooking time: 4 minutes

Each serving (1½ cups) provides

calories 377, total fat 16g, saturated fat 2g, cholesterol 95mg, sodium 272mg, total carbohydrate 24g, dietary fiber 3g, protein 36g

✓✓✓	A, C
✓✓	niacin, B₆
✓	B₁, B₂, E, iron, magnesium, potassium, zinc, copper, fiber

1 First, make the dressing. Put all the ingredients for the dressing into a large salad bowl. Briskly whisk together until completely blended.

2 Toast the pecans and caraway seeds in a small, dry skillet over low heat, stirring constantly, for 4 minutes or until the pecans are golden and you can smell the fragrance (watch carefully). Spread them out on a plate to cool.

3 Cut the turkey into bite-size pieces (you need 4½ cups) and place in the bowl with the dressing. Add the cabbage, carrots, celery, and raisins and toss until all the ingredients are well coated with the dressing. Sprinkle in the toasted pecans and caraway seeds and toss again. Serve immediately, as the red cabbage can discolor the salad.

Healthy tips

- Pecans are a rich source of essential fatty acids, polyunsaturated fats, and dietary fiber.
- Cranberries contain a natural antibiotic that helps prevent *E. coli* bacteria from causing urinary tract infections.
- Red cabbage is an excellent source of vitamin C. It also provides some fiber, plus some vitamin B₆, which is needed to help make red blood cells.

More ideas

- Turkey-apple salad with green cabbage: Substitute 4 cups of shredded green cabbage for the red cabbage (step 3). Use 1 cup of unpeeled red apple pieces instead of the carrots (step 3).
- Turkey and red potato salad: Substitute a honey mustard vinaigrette for the cranberry dressing (step 1). Whisk together ¼ cup of golden honey, ¼ cup of extra virgin olive oil, ¼ cup of apple cider vinegar, 2 tablespoons of fresh lemon juice, 1 tablespoon of Dijon mustard, and 2 teaspoons of finely grated gingerroot. For the salad, omit the red cabbage, carrots, celery, and raisins. Instead use 4 cups of cooked red-skinned potatoes (cut in half), 2 cups of fresh snow peas (steamed for 3 minutes), 2 cups of fresh asparagus tips (steamed for 2 minutes), and 1 cup of sliced green onions. Toss these ingredients with the turkey, pecans, and sesame seeds (step 3). Decorate the salad with 1 cup dried pitted red cherries. Serve this salad warm or at room temperature. It's a perfect salad for a buffet.

Roasted chicken salad with ginger

This creamy yet light chicken salad is ideal for serving as a luncheon or cold buffet dish. Basing the dressing on sour cream mixed with mayonnaise makes it lower in fat than many other creamy dressings while still keeping the richness. Don't be tempted to omit the gingerroot – its subtle flavor makes all the difference.

Makes 6 servings

Roasted chicken salad

1 broiler-fryer chicken, roasted (3½ pounds) or 1½ pounds cooked chicken (boneless and skinless)

3 tablespoons fresh lime juice

2 large green apples, such as Granny Smith

4 celery ribs, thinly sliced (2 cups)

4 ounces ready-to-eat dried apricots, quartered (1 cup)

Ginger cream dressing

⅔ cup reduced-fat sour cream

⅓ cup reduced-calorie mayonnaise

1 tablespoon grated peeled gingerroot

1 teaspoon salt

1 teaspoon freshly ground black pepper

½ cup minced white onion

To decorate

½ cup toasted chopped walnuts

Sprigs of watercress

Preparation time: 25 minutes

Each serving (1½ cups) provides

calories 366, total fat 15g, saturated fat 3g, cholesterol 89mg, sodium 502mg, **total carbohydrate 28g, dietary fiber 4g, protein 33g**

✓✓	A, niacin, B$_6$, E
✓	B$_2$, C, iron, magnesium, potassium, zinc, copper, fiber

1 First, make the salad. If using a whole roasted chicken, remove the meat from the bones and discard the skin and bones. Cut the chicken into bite-size pieces (you need 4½ cups) and place in a large serving bowl.

2 Squeeze the lime juice into a medium-size bowl. Core and cut the apples into ½-inch dice (do not peel) and add to the lime juice in the bowl. Toss until all of the pieces are well coated (this prevents the apples from turning brown in the salad).

3 To the chicken, add the apples and any lime juice remaining in the bowl, the celery, and the apricots. Toss gently until well mixed.

4 Now, make the dressing. In a small bowl, stir together the sour cream, mayonnaise, gingerroot, salt, and pepper. Fold in the onion. Spoon this dressing over the chicken mixture and toss gently until all the pieces are coated well. Sprinkle the toasted walnuts on top of the salad and garnish with the sprigs of watercress.

More ideas

• Smoked turkey salad: Substitute 1½ pounds of cooked smoked turkey (boneless and skinless), cut into bite-size pieces (4½ cups), for the chicken (step 1). Substitute 1 cup of dried pitted cherries for the apricots (step 3).

• Chicken and grape salad: Add 1 cup of red or purple seedless grapes, cut in half, with the apples, celery, and apricots (step 3). Substitute ½ cup of toasted slivered almonds for the walnuts (step 4).

• Chicken and pineapple salad: Add 2 cups of fresh pineapple wedges with the apples, celery, and apricots (step 3).

• Chicken and melon: Substitute 2 cups of honeydew melon balls for the apricots (step 3).

Healthy tips

• This recipe offers a good source of dietary fiber, thanks to the unpeeled apples, celery, and dried apricots. Fiber is essential to keep the digestive tract healthy. The soluble fiber pectin can lower blood cholesterol levels.

• Dried apricots provide a good source of beta-carotene, which the body converts into vitamin A. They are also one of the best fruit sources of iron.

• Some studies indicate that eating a small quantity of walnuts daily, as part of a low-fat diet, can help to reduce high blood cholesterol levels.

Japanese chicken salad

In true Japanese style, the presentation of juicy steamed chicken and clusters of fresh vegetables is a work of art. It's an ideal buffet dish, as the dressing is served separately, so the vegetables stay crisp until they are eaten.

Makes 6 servings

Sesame tahini dressing

3 tablespoons fresh lemon juice

2 tablespoons mirin (rice wine) or saké

2 tablespoons low-sodium soy sauce

2 tablespoons tahini (sesame seed paste)

1 large garlic clove, minced

Pinch of chili powder

Japanese chicken salad

1½ pounds boneless skinless chicken breasts

2 tablespoons mirin (rice wine) or saké

½ teaspoon freshly ground white pepper

1 large cucumber, unpeeled

4 large carrots, peeled

2 large red bell peppers

1 large head Bibb lettuce

½ cup finely shredded basil leaves

½ cup finely shredded mint leaves

8 spring onions, cut in half lengthwise

6 ounces button mushrooms, thinly sliced

Preparation time: 45 minutes

Cooking time: 10 minutes

Each serving provides

calories 214, total fat 4g, saturated fat 1g, cholesterol 69mg, sodium 276mg, total carbohydrate 14g, dietary fiber 3g, protein 28g

✓✓✓	A, niacin, C
✓✓	B₆
✓	B₁, B₂, folate, iron, magnesium, potassium, copper, fiber

1 First, make the dressing. In a small bowl, whisk all of the dressing ingredients together. Pour into a small serving dish.

2 Now, make the salad. To steam the chicken, place the chicken breasts over boiling water in a steamer or on a rack in a shallow skillet with a cover. Sprinkle with the mirin and pepper. Cover and steam for 10 minutes or until the juices of the chicken run clear when a breast is pierced with a fork. Transfer to a plate to cool.

3 Cut the cucumber (do not peel) and the carrots into 3-inch thin matchsticks. Remove the stem, seeds, and membranes from the red pepper and cut into thin 3-inch matchsticks. Separate the lettuce into leaves and arrange at one end of a large platter. Scatter the shredded basil and mint over the lettuce and the rest of the platter.

4 Cut the chicken into thin slices and place on the lettuce. Arrange the cucumber, carrots, peppers, onions, and mushrooms attractively on the platter. Serve with the dressing in a small bowl.

More ideas

● Oriental chicken salad with plum dressing: Reduce the carrots to 2 (step 3). Add a mound of 4 cups of fresh bean sprouts on the platter plus a cluster of 1 cup sliced water chestnuts, and another cluster of 1 cup of drained canned baby corn (step 4). To make the dressing, substitute ⅓ cup of bottled plum sauce for the mirin and 2 tablespoons of toasted sesame oil for the tahini (step 1). Top with 2 tablespoons of toasted sesame seeds.

● Tahini tip: Popular in Middle Eastern cooking, this thick oily paste is made from crushed sesame seeds. If you are not able to find it in your market, toast ¼ cup sesame seeds in a small skillet over high heat for a few minutes, stirring constantly and watching them closely so they do not burn. Then process the seeds with a little sesame oil in a food processor (or mash in a mortar with a pestle) until a paste forms.

Healthy tips

● Because all of the vegetables are eaten raw, this salad offers excellent amounts of vitamin C, which helps the body absorb the iron from the chicken. The vegetables are also an excellent source of fiber and of beta-carotene, which with vitamin C, play a role in protecting against cancer.

● Mushrooms are low in calories and are fat-free. They provide fair amounts of niacin, riboflavin, and copper. Mushrooms are a fair source of selenium, an antioxidant that works with vitamin E to protect cells from oxidative damage.

Poultry in a Hurry

Sautés and stir-fries — fast to fix

CERTAIN CUTS OF POULTRY COOK QUICKLY, making them the perfect pick when you have little time to cook. Stir-fry lean duck breasts the Chinese way, with plenty of tender-crisp vegetables, fresh sprouts, and fragrant juicy pears. Grill curried chicken breasts over very hot coals, the Indian tandoori way, then serve with a cucumber raita salad. Quickly pan-fry thin *escalopes* of turkey and top in the French manner with a citrus and sweet onion sauce. Sauté boneless chicken thighs in the traditional style of the Mediterranean with marinated artichokes, red peppers, olives, and white wine. Or turn leftover chicken into that all-American favorite of skillet potato hash.

Spiced stir-fried duck

Take strips of duck and stir-fry them in the Chinese tradition with onions, water chestnuts, bok choy, and bean sprouts. And for an unusual sweet touch, add some chunks of juicy fresh pear. Stir-fry them in a wok or your heaviest deepest skillet over a high heat, for just a few minutes, then serve over cooked Chinese noodles.

Makes 6 servings

1½ pounds boneless duck breasts

2 teaspoons five-spice powder

4 ribs celery, plus a few leaves to decorate

8 ounces small white onions

2 large juicy pears

1 cup sliced canned water chestnuts
(one 8-ounce can)

8 ounces bok choy (also known as pak choy)

8 ounces bean sprouts

2 tablespoons sunflower oil

3 tablespoons rice vinegar or sherry vinegar

3 tablespoons low-sodium soy sauce

2 tablespoons golden honey

To serve

6 cups cooked Chinese noodles or spaghetti
(optional)

Preparation time: 30 minutes
Cooking time: 10 minutes

Each serving provides

calories 312, total fat 8g, saturated fat 1g, cholesterol 162mg, sodium 418mg, total carbohydrate 26g, dietary fiber 4g, protein 35g

✓✓✓	niacin, C
✓✓	iron
✓	B_2, B_6, folate, potassium, copper, fiber

1 Remove the skin and all fat from the duck breasts, then cut them across the grain into long strips, 1 inch wide. Sprinkle with the five-spice powder and toss to coat. Set aside.

2 Now, prepare the vegetables. Thinly slice the ribs of celery (you need 2 cups). Peel and thinly slice the onions (you need 1 cup). Peel, core, and cut the pears into bite-size pieces (you need 2 cups). Drain the water chestnuts. Shred the bok choy (you need 3 cups). Wash and drain the bean sprouts (you need 1½ cups).

3 Now, prepare the stir-fry. Heat a wok or heavy-based frying pan over high heat until piping hot. Add the oil, swirling the wok to coat the bottom and sides. Add the duck breasts and stir-fry for 2 minutes. Then add the celery and onions and continue to stir-fry for 3 minutes or until the celery and onions have softened. Add the pears and water chestnuts and stir just to mix.

4 In a cup, whisk the vinegar, soy sauce, and honey and add to the wok. Heat until the liquid is bubbling and stir-fry 2 minutes more. Add the bok choy and bean sprouts and stir-fry 1 minute more or just until the bok choy and sprouts wilt. Decorate with the celery leaves and serve with the Chinese noodles, if you wish.

Healthy tips

● Removing the skin and fat from duck lowers the fat content substantially. Ounce per ounce, a skinless duck breast contains 77% less fat than one with both its skin and fat intact.

● Dark green leafy vegetables, such as bok choy, provide a good source of vitamin C, as well as vitamin B_6, folate, and niacin.

● Bean sprouts are a good source of vitamin C and also offer B vitamins.

● Water chestnuts are low in calories and have no fat. They provide fair amounts of protein and vitamin C.

More ideas

● Orange stir-fried duck: Use 1 teaspoon of ground anise instead of the five-star powder (step 1). Substitute 2 cups of fresh orange sections for the pears (steps 2 and 3). Stir 2 tablespoons of fresh orange juice into the sauce with the vinegar (step 4).

● Spiced duck in plum sauce: Substitute 2 cups of peeled ripe plum slices for the pears (steps 2 and 3). Stir 2 tablespoons of bottled plum sauce into the sauce with the vinegar (step 4).

● Spicy stir-fried chicken: Substitute 1½ pounds of boneless skinless chicken breasts (cut into strips) for the duck breasts.

poultry in a hurry

Turkey *escalope* sauté with citrus and sweet onion sauce

No longer do you have to roast a whole turkey to enjoy this delicious bird. Look in your market for turkey breast steaks. Pound them thin into escalopes, *sauté them quickly and serve with a honey, citrus, and sweet onion sauce.*

Makes 4 servings

Citrus and sweet onion sauce

2 tablespoons grated orange zest

½ cup fresh orange juice

2 teaspoons grated lemon zest

¼ cup fresh lemon juice

3 tablespoons golden honey

½ teaspoon freshly ground black pepper

Turkey *escalope* sauté

4 small boneless skinless turkey breast
  steaks (4 ounces each)

1 teaspoon salt

1 pound string beans or French haricots verts

2 tablespoons unsalted butter

1 extra-large yellow onion, slivered (1½ cups)

2 large shallots, sliced (½ cup)

2 large garlic cloves, minced

Preparation time: 15 minutes

Cooking time: 13 minutes

Each serving (1 escalope) provides

calories 315, **total fat** 7g, **saturated fat** 4g, **cholesterol** 86mg, **sodium** 587mg, **total carbohydrate** 37g, **dietary fiber** 4g, **protein** 29g

✓✓✓	C
✓✓	A, niacin, B$_6$
✓	B$_1$, B$_2$, folate, calcium, iron, magnesium, potassium, zinc, copper, fiber

1 First, assemble the sauce. In a small bowl, whisk the orange zest and juice, the lemon zest and juice, the honey, and pepper; set aside.

2 Now, flatten out the turkey steaks. Place the steaks, 1 at a time, between 2 sheets of plastic wrap and pound them with a meat mallet to ¼ inch thick. Or, ask your butcher to pound them for you. Sprinkle both sides of steaks with ½ teaspoon of the salt.

3 To cook the string beans, half-fill a medium-size saucepan with water, add the remaining salt, and bring to a boil over medium-high heat. Add the beans and cook for 3 minutes or just until the beans turn bright green. Drain, transfer to a platter, and keep warm.

4 Meanwhile, in a large nonstick skillet, melt the butter over medium-high heat. Add the onion, shallots, and garlic; sauté for 2 minutes or just until the onion is transparent, but not brown. Using a slotted spoon, transfer to a plate.

5 Sauté turkey *escalopes* in the same skillet for 3 minutes on each side. Arrange on top of the beans; keep hot. Pour the sauce into the skillet, add the onion mixture, and boil 2 minutes. Spoon over turkey *escalopes* and serve.

More ideas

● Sautéed duck breasts with raspberry-citrus sauce: Make the sauce as directed (step 1). Substitute 4 boneless skinless duck breasts (a total of 1½ pounds) for the turkey steaks. Remove their skins but do not flatten them (step 2). For duck breasts with pink centers, sauté for 3 minutes on each side; for well done duck, 1 or 2 minutes longer on each side (step 5). After the sauce and onion mixture has simmered for 2 minutes, stir in 1 cup of fresh raspberries and heat through (step 4).

● Turkey *escalopes* with honey-glazed vegetables: Cook 1 cup of peeled baby carrots (cut in half lengthwise) with the string beans; drain. Toss with 2 tablespoons *each* of honey, lemon juice, and butter (step 3) and keep hot.

Healthy tips

● Turkey contains even less fat than chicken, making it one of the lowest fat meats available.

● All citrus fruits are an excellent source of vitamin C. This vitamin helps reduce the risk of cataracts, and is essential for healthy gums and teeth.

Chicken and artichoke sauté

On the Mediterranean coast, artichokes, peppers, and olives often team up in the same dish to create traditional fare. Simmer them in a lemony white wine sauce, as the perfect accompaniment for sautéed chicken thighs.

Makes 6 servings

⅓ cup all-purpose flour

1 tablespoon chopped fresh thyme leaves

½ teaspoon salt

½ teaspoon freshly ground black pepper

12 small boneless skinless chicken thighs
(2¼ pounds / 3 ounces each after boning)

3 tablespoons extra-virgin olive oil

Artichoke-red pepper sauté

1½ cups bottled, marinated artichoke hearts

2 large red bell peppers

1 large garlic clove, minced

½ cup pitted black olives, cut in half

⅓ cup dry white wine

⅔ cup chicken stock, preferably homemade
(see page 23)

2 teaspoons grated lemon zest

To decorate

Sprigs of fresh thyme

2 large lemons, cut into 4 wedges each

Preparation time: 20 minutes

Cooking time: 25 minutes

Each serving (2 thighs) provides

calories 375, total fat 19g, saturated fat 3g, cholesterol 141mg, sodium 637mg, total carbohydrate 14g, dietary fiber 1g, protein 36g

✓✓✓	niacin, C
✓✓	B₆
✓	B₁, B₂, iron, magnesium, potassium, zinc

1 First, sauté the chicken. Preheat the oven to its lowest setting (warm). In a large self-closing plastic bag, shake the flour, thyme, salt, and pepper. Add the chicken thighs to the bag, a few at a time, and shake until they are lightly and evenly coated. Remove the chicken to a plate, shaking off and discarding any excess flour.

2 In a large nonstick skillet, heat the oil over medium-high heat. Add the chicken thighs and sauté for about 3 minutes on each side or until they are golden brown. (If the skillet is not large enough to hold the thighs in a single layer, sauté them in batches.)

3 Reduce the heat to medium and cook 12 minutes more or until the juices of the chicken run clear when a thigh is pierced with a fork. Transfer the thighs to a heatproof platter and place in the oven to keep warm.

4 Now, prepare the artichoke-red pepper sauté. Drain the artichokes well. Remove the stems, seeds, and membranes of the bell peppers, then cut the peppers into thin strips. Add the garlic to the same skillet and cook over medium-high heat for 30 seconds or just until soft. Add the artichokes and red peppers, and sauté for 5 minutes or just until the peppers are crisp-tender. Stir in the black olives.

5 Add the wine and let the vegetables simmer, stirring constantly, until the wine has almost evaporated. Stir in the stock and lemon zest, bring to a boil, and let boil, uncovered, until the liquid has reduced by about one-half. Taste the sauté and season with additional salt and pepper, if you wish.

6 Transfer the chicken thighs from the oven to a large serving platter and spoon the artichoke and pepper mixture alongside. Decorate with thyme sprigs and lemon wedges, and serve.

Healthy tips

● Artichokes are not only low in calories and fat, but are also a good source of vitamin C and folate.

● Although olives have a high fat content, most of this fat is the monounsaturated kind. This is the type of fat that is believed to be the healthiest to eat.

● Invest in a good-quality nonstick frying pan. It lets you sauté poultry and vegetables with less oil.

poultry in a hurry

More ideas

• Chicken breast sauté: Substitute 1 pound of boneless skinless chicken breasts for the chicken thighs (step 1). Reduce the sautéing time to 6 to 8 minutes, depending upon the thickness of the chicken breasts. Be careful not to overcook them (steps 2 and 3).

• Chicken with zucchini sauté: Omit the artichokes. Sauté 2 cups of sliced mushrooms with the garlic, then add 2 cups of zucchini slices with the red pepper strips (step 4). Decorate with ¼ cup fresh basil leaves instead of the sprigs of fresh thyme (step 6).

• Chicken with asparagus: Substitute 2 cups of fresh asparagus tips for the artichokes (step 4).

Polenta with turkey and wild mushroom sauté

Take two different kinds of mushrooms — white button ones and velvety smoky shiitakes. Sauté them in butter with a little tomato paste and a splash of sherry. Add chunks of cooked turkey, then smooth out the flavors with some light cream. Serve with soft polenta on the side. It's a marvelous way to dress up leftover turkey.

Makes 4 servings

Polenta

4 cups chicken stock, preferably homemade (see page 23)

1¼ cups instant polenta

½ cup finely chopped flat-leaf parsley

Salt and freshly ground black pepper (optional)

Turkey and mushroom sauté

2 tablespoons unsalted butter

1 tablespoon extra virgin olive oil

1 small yellow onion, finely chopped (½ cup)

3 large garlic cloves, minced

8 ounces shiitake mushrooms, sliced (3 cups)

8 ounces white mushrooms, sliced vertically (3 cups)

⅓ cup dry sherry

2 tablespoons tomato paste

1 pound cooked turkey breast (boneless and skinless), cut into bite-size pieces (3 cups)

⅓ cup light cream

¾ teaspoon freshly ground black pepper

¼ teaspoon salt

To decorate

Sprigs of flat-leaf parsley

Preparation time: 30 minutes

Cooking time: 20 minutes

1 First, start preparing the polenta. In a large saucepan, bring the stock to a full boil over high heat. While stirring constantly, gradually pour in the polenta. When all the polenta has been added, stir in the parsley. Lower the heat to medium and cook for 2 minutes or according to the package directions, stirring constantly, until the polenta is thick and all of the stock has been absorbed. Season to taste with salt and pepper if you wish. Cover and keep hot.

2 Now, prepare the turkey sauté. In a large skillet, heat the butter and oil over medium-high heat. Add the onion and garlic; sauté for 3 minutes or until the onion is translucent but not brown.

3 Add both the shiitakes and the white mushrooms to the skillet and sauté 4 minutes more or just until the mushrooms soften and their juices begin to show. Stir in the sherry and tomato paste, then gently stir in the turkey. Reduce the heat to low; heat through.

4 Add the cream, pepper, and salt to the turkey and mushroom mixture and heat 1 minute more or until hot (do not let boil). Serve the turkey sauté with the polenta alongside. Decorate with parsley sprigs.

Healthy tips

• Mushrooms are fat-free and low in calories; ⅓ of a cup has only 10 calories.

• Polenta is low in fat, contains no cholesterol, and is a fair source of fiber.

Another idea

• Sautéed turkey, mushrooms, and peppers: Instead of the polenta, substitute a 6-ounce package of long-grain white rice and wild-rice mix and prepare according to the package directions (step 1). Add the parsley and ½ cup of toasted finely chopped pecans (step 1). Add 2 cups of thin red bell pepper strips with the onion and garlic (step 2). Sauté for 5 minutes (instead of 3 minutes) or just until the peppers begin to wilt. Substitute ½ cup of Marsala wine for the dry sherry (step 3).

Each serving provides

calories 523, **total fat** 17g, **saturated fat** 7g, **cholesterol** 125mg, **sodium** 715mg, **total carbohydrate** 43g, **dietary fiber** 5g, **protein** 46g

✓✓✓	niacin, copper
✓✓	B_2, B_6, C, iron
✓	A, B_1, folate, calcium, magnesium, potassium, zinc, fiber

Tandoori grilled chicken breasts

In India, the tandoor oven is a barrel-shaped clay oven, heated by hot coals, to such a high temperature it sears meats in seconds, without adding fat. At home, a grill works fine too. Here, breasts of chicken are seasoned with Indian spices from curry powder and garam masala. Serve raita, the creamy yogurt-vegetable salad, alongside.

Makes 6 servings

Indian-spiced marinade
½ cup plain low-fat yogurt
2 tablespoons tomato paste
1 tablespoon grated peeled gingerroot
1 tablespoon curry powder
2 teaspoons garam masala
1 large garlic clove, minced

Tandoori grilled chicken
6 boneless skinless chicken breast halves
   (5 ounces each)
Sunflower oil for brushing grill

Raita
1 large cucumber
1½ cups plain low-fat yogurt
1 large tomato, finely chopped (1 cup)
½ teaspoon ground coriander
½ teaspoon ground cumin
Pinch of cayenne pepper
Pinch of salt

To decorate
2 large lemons or limes, cut in wedges
Sprigs of fresh coriander

Preparation time: 30 minutes
Marinating time: 30 minutes or overnight
Cooking time: 15 minutes

1 To make the marinade, process all of the marinade ingredients in a food processor or blender for about 30 seconds or until blended. Or, if you do not have this equipment, simply whisk together all of the ingredients in a small bowl. Transfer to a large shallow bowl that is large enough to hold the chicken breasts in a single layer.

2 Score 2 slits on each side of the chicken breasts. Place them in the marinade, turning to coat and rubbing the marinade into the slits. Cover with plastic wrap and let marinate in the refrigerator for 30 minutes (or, if you have time, marinate overnight).

3 Meanwhile, make the raita. Cut the cucumber into half lengthwise (do not peel) and remove the seeds with a spoon. Now, grate the cucumber into a medium-size bowl and squeeze out as much juice as possible with your hands (discard the juice). Add the remaining ingredients for the raita and mix well; transfer to a serving bowl and keep cold in the refrigerator.

4 To cook the chicken, preheat the grill or broiler to high. Remove the chicken from the marinade. Discard the marinade. Brush the grill rack with oil, then place the chicken breasts on top. Grill or broil 6" from the heat for 12 minutes, turning several times, until the juices of the chicken run clear when a breast is pierced with a fork (do not worry if the outsides of the chicken breasts look slightly charred).

5 Transfer the chicken breasts to a serving plate. Decorate with the lemon or lime wedges and the sprigs of coriander. Serve with the raita in a separate serving dish, on the side.

Healthy tips

- Chicken is a low-fat source of protein, plus this marinade adds very little extra fat.
- Yogurt is an excellent source of protein and calcium, needed for healthy bones and teeth. It also provides fair amounts of phosphorus and vitamins B_2 and B_{12}, as well as beneficial bacteria.

Each serving provides
calories 242, total fat 5g, saturated fat 2g, cholesterol 91mg, sodium 212mg, total carbohydrate 11g, dietary fiber 1g, protein 37g

✓✓✓	niacin
✓✓	B_6
✓	B_2, B_{12}, C, calcium, iron, magnesium, potassium, zinc

More ideas

• Tandoori chicken kebabs: First, cut the chicken breasts into 1¼-inch cubes, then place them in the marinade (step 2). Soak 8 bamboo skewers in cold water. Cut 1 large zucchini (do not peel) in circles, ½ inch thick. Cut 1 large red bell pepper and 1 large yellow bell pepper into 1¼-inch cubes. Parboil the vegetables in boiling water for 3 minutes or just until crisp-tender. Alternately thread the chicken and vegetables on the 8 skewers. Grill or broil the kebabs for only 8 to 10 minutes (step 4).

• Spicy onion raita: Use the 1½ cups of low-fat yogurt for the raita and the 1 cup of finely chopped tomato, but omit the other ingredients (step 3). Instead, mix in 1 cup of finely chopped sweet Vidalia onions or thinly sliced green onions, ⅓ cup of slivered fresh mint leaves, 2 tablespoons of slivered fresh coriander leaves, and 1 small minced green chili (discard seeds and membrane). Heat a dry frying pan over high heat, add 2 teaspoons of cumin seeds, and sauté, stirring constantly, until they give off their aroma. Sprinkle on top of the raita.

• In a hurry? If you don't have the time to prepare the raita, serve the chicken breasts with a simple salad of chopped tomatoes, thin cucumber slices, and red onion slivers. Drizzle with white wine vinegar, a splash of sunflower oil, and a sprinkle of slivered coriander leaves.

Chicken livers sautéed with sage

Quickly sauté chicken livers with fresh mushrooms, then spark up the dish with a splash of balsamic vinegar, shreds of fresh sage leaves, and a little dry sherry. Spoon the livers over toasted French bread for a fast, but special, supper. Another day, serve them the old-fashioned way: over a mound of homemade mashed potatoes.

Makes 4 servings

2 tablespoons unsalted butter

2 tablespoons extra virgin olive oil

8 slices French bread, 1 inch thick

1 small red onion, finely chopped (½ cup)

2 garlic cloves, minced

1 pound chicken livers

8 ounces white mushrooms, quartered
   (3 cups)

3 tablespoons balsamic vinegar

2 tablespoons shredded fresh sage leaves

¾ teaspoon salt

¾ teaspoon freshly ground black pepper

2 tablespoons dry sherry

To decorate

Sprigs of fresh sage

Preparation time: 25 minutes

Cooking time: 20 minutes

Each serving provides

calories 407, total fat 18g, saturated fat 6g, cholesterol 462mg, sodium 746mg, total carbohydrate 35g, dietary fiber 1g, protein 23g

✓✓✓	A, B$_2$, B$_{12}$, folate
✓✓	B$_1$, niacin, B$_6$, C, iron, zinc, copper
✓	magnesium, potassium

1 Preheat the oven to 350°F. In a large skillet, melt the butter and heat the oil over medium heat; remove the skillet from the heat. Brush both sides of the bread slices with about half of the butter-oil mixture. Place on a baking sheet. Bake for 10 minutes or until golden brown, turning the bread slices over about halfway through.

2 Meanwhile, reheat the remaining butter-oil mixture over medium-high heat in the same skillet. Add the onion and garlic and sauté for 5 minutes or until softened.

3 Add the chicken livers and sauté for 3 minutes. Add the mushrooms and continue sautéing 5 minutes more or until both the livers and the mushrooms are brown (don't worry if the livers break up a little as they cook).

4 Add the vinegar, sage, salt, and pepper to the liver mixture in the skillet. Reduce the heat to medium-low and cook 3 minutes more or until the livers are just cooked through. Stir in the sherry and remove from the heat.

5 Place 2 slices of bread on each of 4 individual plates. Spoon the chicken livers on top and decorate with sprigs of fresh sage.

Healthy tips

• Like all liver, chicken livers are a rich source of iron, which helps prevent anemia.

• Garlic (along with leeks, onions, and chives) contains allicin, which reduces blood cholesterol levels. It also lowers blood pressure, possibly reducing the risk of heart attacks and strokes. Garlic contains other compounds that may reduce the risk of colon cancer.

More ideas

• Sautéed chicken livers over homemade mashed potatoes: Instead of toasting French bread (step 1), mash 4 medium-size cooked all-purpose potatoes with 2 tablespoons of unsalted butter and ¼ cup of low-fat milk (2% milkfat), adding a little more milk if necessary to make the potatoes extra fluffy. Fold in 2 tablespoons of minced chives. Spoon the chicken livers on top (step 5).

• Chicken livers Provençale: Substitute ¼ cup of dry red wine for the balsamic vinegar and 1 teaspoon dried herbes de Provence for the slivered sage leaves (step 4). Serve with a mixture of cooked long-grain and wild rice.

• Sautéed chicken livers with fresh marjoram: Substitute 3 tablespoons of chopped fresh marjoram leaves for the chopped sage (step 4). Decorate with sprigs of fresh marjoram instead of the sprigs of sage (step 5).

Chicken and sweet potato hash

Hash is an all-American favorite. Here, it's made with bites of roasted chicken, cubes of sweet potatoes, kernels of sweet corn, and bits of dried tomatoes. Top it off with a simple sour cream sauce and serve with rustic country bread and a crisp spinach salad. For variety, try the spicy version made with white potatoes, apples, and curry.

Makes 4 servings

Hash
1 pound sweet potatoes, peeled

12 ounces all-purpose white potatoes, peeled

2 tablespoons sunflower oil

8 ounces leeks, sliced (2 cups)

1½ cups fresh or thawed frozen yellow corn kernels

1 pound cooked chicken breasts (boneless and skinless), cut into bite-size pieces

8 sun-dried tomatoes packed in oil, drained and chopped (½ cup)

1 teaspoon paprika

1 teaspoon salt

Sour cream sauce
1 cup reduced-fat sour cream

1 small garlic clove, minced

½ teaspoon paprika

Preparation time: 15 minutes
Cooking time: 20 minutes

Each serving provides
calories 600, **total fat** 18g, **saturated fat** 3g, **cholesterol** 115mg, **sodium** 725mg, **total carbohydrate** 65g, **dietary fiber** 2g, **protein** 43g

✓✓✓	A, niacin, B₆, C
✓✓	B₂, potassium
✓	B₁, folate, calcium, iron, magnesium, zinc, copper

1 Cut the sweet potatoes and potatoes into bite-size chunks (you need 5 cups of potatoes). Half-fill a saucepan with water and bring to a boil over high heat. Add the potatoes, return to a boil and boil for 3 minutes. Transfer to a colander, drain well, and set aside.

2 Heat the oil in a large nonstick frying pan and add the leeks, corn, and potato mixture. Cook over medium-high heat, stirring frequently, for 4 minutes or just until the vegetables begin to brown.

3 Add the chicken pieces, sun-dried tomatoes, paprika, and salt; mix thoroughly. Continue cooking 4 minutes more, pressing the mixture down well to make a cake in the pan. Using a spatula, turn the mixture over in chunks, until brown and crispy on all sides.

4 Now, make the sauce. Place all of the sauce ingredients in a small bowl and stir to mix. Serve portions of hash and top generously with the sauce.

More ideas
• Garden vegetable potato hash: Sauté 1 cup of chopped green bell pepper with the leeks, corn, and potato mixture (step 2). Omit the sun-dried tomatoes (step 3).

• Chicken and apple hash: Increase the white potatoes to 1 pound (3 cups bite-size chunks); omit sweet potatoes (step 1). Omit the leeks and corn. Instead, sauté 2 cups of chopped yellow onions, 1½ cups of chopped peeled apple, and 1 cup of chopped red pepper with the potatoes (step 2). Omit the sun-dried tomatoes. Stir in 2 tablespoons of mango chutney and 1 tablespoon of curry paste with the chicken, paprika, and salt (step 3).

• Blue-plate hash special: Increase the white potatoes to 1 pound (3 cups bite-size chunks); omit the sweet potatoes (step 1). Omit the sun-dried tomatoes; stir in 2 teaspoons of Worcestershire sauce (step 3).

Healthy tips
• Sweet potatoes are an excellent source of beta-carotene, an antioxidant that helps prevent the cancer-causing cell damage of free radicals. Additionally, sweet potatoes provide excellent amounts of vitamins C, niacin, and B₆, as well as good amounts of potassium. Their flavor comes from an enzyme that converts starches to sugar.

• Both potatoes and sweet potatoes contain complex carbohydrates, which the body metabolizes into glucose (blood sugar) as its primary source of energy.

Main Course Poultry

From oven roasts to round-the-world favorites

ROASTING A BIRD, WHETHER STUFFED OR UNSTUFFED, is one of the simplest ways to serve dinner, often leaving enough leftovers to enjoy later. Simply tuck garlic and fresh herbs beneath the skin, squeeze a lemon inside the cavity, and roast until juicy. Or adopt ways of cooking poultry from around the world. Glaze a duck crisp and spicy, as in China; braise chicken fillets in Burgundy wine, as in France; stuff a turkey with spicy couscous, as in the Middle East; sauté in Marsala, as in Sicily; and barbecue with a hot jerk sauce, as in the Caribbean.

Roasted herb and garlic chicken

The next time you roast a chicken, try replacing the traditional butter basting sauce with this cream cheese and fresh herb seasoning paste that you push underneath the skin. Stuff the cavity with a large fresh lemon. Then baste with a dry white wine as the bird cooks. For the gravy, just thicken the pan juices with a little cornstarch.

Makes 6 servings

Roasted chicken

1 whole roasting chicken (about 5 pounds)

1 teaspoon freshly ground black pepper

½ teaspoon salt

2 teaspoons grated lemon zest

1 large lemon

1 cup fresh coriander leaves

1 cup fresh parsley

2 large garlic cloves, peeled

¼ cup reduced-fat cream cheese (Neufchâtel)

3 tablespoons reduced-fat sour cream

⅔ cup dry white wine

Chicken stock or chicken broth (about 1 cup)

2 tablespoons cornstarch

¼ cup cold water

To decorate

Lemon slices

Sprigs of fresh coriander and parsley

Preparation time: 30 minutes

Roasting time: 1¾ hours

Each serving (with skin) provides

calories 470, total fat 26g, saturated fat 8g, cholesterol 143mg, **sodium** 402mg, **total carbohydrate** 8g, **dietary fiber** 0g, **protein** 44g

✓✓✓	niacin, C
✓✓	B₆
✓	A, B₂, iron, magnesium, potassium, zinc

1 Preheat the oven to 425°F and set out a roasting pan and rack. Wash the chicken inside and out with cold running water; discard the giblets and neck. Sprinkle the large cavity with half of the pepper and salt. Grate the zest from the lemon and sprinkle 1 teaspoon of zest into the cavity. Cut the lemon in half. Holding the chicken on a slant, squeeze the lemon juice inside the cavity. Stuff the 2 lemon halves inside.

2 Place the chicken breast-side up. Starting at the neck end, ease your fingers gently under the skin to loosen the skin over the breasts and thighs (be careful not to tear the skin).

3 In a food processor or blender, process the coriander, parsley, and garlic until finely chopped. Add the cream cheese and sour cream, and the remaining pepper, salt, and lemon zest; process a few seconds more to mix. Push the herb cheese under the skin, easing it along so that it covers the breasts and thighs evenly in a thin layer.

4 Truss the chicken and insert a roasting thermometer in its thigh, then place on the rack in the pan. Pour the wine over the chicken and roast at 425°F for 30 minutes. Lower the oven temperature to 350°F and continue roasting the chicken, without covering, basting frequently with the pan juices,

for 1¼ hours or until the thermometer registers 180°F and the juices of the chicken run clear when a thigh is pierced with a fork.

5 Carefully lift the chicken in the roasting pan, tilting it so the juices run out of the cavity into the pan; let it stand on a carving board 10 minutes.

6 Meanwhile, pour the pan drippings into a heatproof measuring cup and skim off the fat. Add enough chicken stock to make 2 cups of liquid and pour back into the roasting pan. In a cup, dissolve the cornstarch in the water and whisk into the drippings. Bring to a boil over high heat, scraping up the browned bits from the bottom of the pan. Boil for 2 minutes or until the gravy thickens.

7 Carve the chicken (leave the skin on). Decorate with lemon slices and sprigs of coriander and parsley. Serve with the pan gravy.

Healthy tips

● Ounce for ounce, cooked chicken breast without its skin has 16% fewer calories and 54% less fat than cooked chicken breast with its skin.

● Chicken is an excellent source of protein and a good source of niacin.

More ideas

● Roasted chicken with wild-rice stuffing: First, cook a 6-ounce package of long-grain white and wild-rice mix, according to package directions; toss in ½ cup of toasted chopped pecans. Then, prepare the chicken, substituting orange zest and juice for the lemon zest and juice; discard the orange halves. Stuff the cavity with the cooked rice mixture (step 1). Prepare and roast the chicken as in steps 2 through 7.

● Roasted chicken with red wine: Omit cream cheese mixture (step 3). Stuff ½ cup of thin peeled Granny Smith apple slices and ½ cup of yellow onion slivers under the skin. Substitute ⅔ cup of red wine for the white wine.

Turkey with lemon couscous

You don't have to wait until Thanksgiving to enjoy delicious roast turkey. Frozen turkeys, and often fresh ones too, are available year-round. The smaller 10 to 12-pound turkey hens are exceptionally juicy and tender — ideal for serving ten people. Use the turkey carcass and any meat left over for soup (see page 28).

Makes 10 servings

Lemon couscous stuffing

5 large lemons
2½ cups hot chicken or turkey stock
1 cup boiling water
¾ cup ready-to-eat dried apricots, chopped
¼ cup slivered fresh mint leaves, plus sprigs
1 teaspoon ground cinnamon
1 teaspoon ground cumin
1 teaspoon ground turmeric
2 packages instant couscous
    (10 ounces each)

Roasted turkey

1 whole turkey, fresh or frozen and thawed
    (about 10 to 12 pounds)
1 teaspoon salt
1 teaspoon freshly ground black pepper
¾ cup dry white wine
3 tablespoons cornstarch
⅓ cup cold water

Preparation time: 30 minutes
Roasting time: 3½ hours

Each serving (without skin) provides
calories 636, total fat 11g, saturated fat 4g,
cholesterol 159mg, sodium 437mg, total
carbohydrate 60g, dietary fiber 10g, protein 70g

✓✓✓	niacin, B₆, C
✓✓	B₂, iron, potassium, zinc, copper, fiber
✓	B₁, B₁₂, calcium, magnesium

1 Preheat the oven to 325°F and set out a roasting pan and rack. Cut the lemons in half lengthwise. Gently squeeze the juice into a measuring cup; discard the seeds and the membranes. Cut a thin slice off the base of each lemon shell so that it stands firmly. Set aside the 10 shells.

2 In a medium-size saucepan, mix 1½ cups of the stock, the boiling water, ¼ cup of the lemon juice, the apricots, the slivered mint leaves (save sprigs for decorating), the cinnamon, cumin, and turmeric; bring to a boil over high heat. Stir in the couscous. Remove from the heat, cover, and let stand for 5 minutes or until the couscous has absorbed all the liquid.

3 Wash the turkey inside and out with cold running water; discard the giblets and neck. Sprinkle both the small and large cavities with the salt and pepper. Stuff both cavities with the couscous and truss the turkey.

4 Insert a roasting thermometer into a thigh of the turkey, then place on the rack in the pan. Pour the wine and the remaining lemon juice over the turkey, cover with the top to the roasting pan or with buttered foil. Roast the bird, basting frequently with the pan juices, for 3 hours. Uncover the pan. Continue roasting the bird 30 minutes more or until the turkey is golden brown, a thermometer registers 180°F, and the juices of the turkey run clear when a thigh is pierced with a fork. Transfer the bird to a carving board and let it stand for 10 minutes.

5 Meanwhile, pour the pan drippings into a heatproof measuring cup and skim off the fat. Add the remaining 1 cup of chicken stock, plus water if necessary, to make 3 cups of liquid, then return the mixture to the roasting pan. In a cup, dissolve the cornstarch in the ⅓ cup cold water and whisk into the drippings. Bring to a boil over high heat, scraping up the browned bits from the bottom of the pan, and boil for 2 minutes or until the gravy thickens.

6 Stuff the lemon shells with some of the couscous. Carve the turkey, discarding the skin. Decorate with the lemon shells, any extra couscous, and sprigs of mint. Serve with pan gravy.

Healthy tip
• Couscous is low in fat and high in starch, a carbohydrate. It scores low on the glycemic index scale, which means that it breaks down slowly in the body, releasing energy gradually into the bloodstream.

main course poultry

82

More ideas

• Roasted turkey with old-fashioned bread stuffing: Omit the lemon shells and couscous stuffing (steps 1 and 2). Replace with 6 cups of dry bread stuffing and prepare according to package directions. Into the stuffing, mix in 1½ cups of crumbled cooked chicken sausage, 1 cup of sautéed chopped celery, 1 cup of sautéed chopped yellow onion, ⅓ cup of chopped parsley, 1 tablespoon of slivered fresh sage leaves, and 1 teaspoon of fresh thyme leaves. Stir in 1 beaten large egg and stuff the turkey with this mixture. To baste, use ⅓ cup of fresh lemon juice with the wine (step 4).

• Roasted turkey with corn-bread stuffing: Omit the lemon shells and the couscous stuffing (steps 1 and 2). Replace with 6 cups of dry corn-bread stuffing and prepare the stuffing according to package directions. Into the stuffing, mix in 1 cup of sautéed chopped celery, 1 cup of sautéed chopped yellow onion, 1 cup of bite-size, peeled apple chunks, ⅓ cup of chopped parsley, 1 teaspoon of poultry seasoning, and 1 teaspoon ground nutmeg. Stir in 1 beaten large egg and stuff the turkey with this mixture. Use ⅓ cup of fresh lemon juice with the wine for basting (step 4).

Pheasant with leeks and lentils

Pheasant has very little fat. Here, it's wrapped in prosciutto to help keep it moist during cooking. Roast it on top of leeks and lentils for the perfect accompaniment. If you're unable to find pheasant, substitute Cornish hens.

Makes 6 servings

2 large yellow onions

2 pheasants, dressed (about 2¼ pounds each), or 6 Cornish game hens (about 1¼ to 1½ pounds each), giblets removed

3 large oranges, halved

2 tablespoons Dijon mustard

Sprigs of fresh sage (5 inches)

4 ounces sliced prosciutto

1¼ cups lentils

1 large leek, sliced (2 cups)

4 ounces ready-to-eat dried apricot halves, quartered (1 cup)

Sprigs fresh thyme (5 ounces)

2 large garlic cloves, minced

2 cups apple cider

1½ cups chicken stock, or more if needed, or low-sodium chicken broth

To garnish

1 large orange, cut into 6 wedges

Preparation time: 30 minutes

Roasting time: 1½ hours

Each serving provides

calories 561, total fat 16g, saturated fat 4g, cholesterol 113mg, sodium 489mg, total carbohydrate 57g, dietary fiber 9g, protein 49g

✓✓✓	niacin, B$_6$, C
✓✓	B$_1$, B$_2$, folate, iron, potassium, copper, fiber
✓	A, B$_{12}$, calcium, magnesium

1 First, preheat the oven to 375°F. Peel the onions and cut each into 6 equal wedges. Stuff each pheasant with 3 orange halves and 6 onion wedges or stuff each Cornish hen with 1 orange half and 2 onion wedges. Spread the mustard over the breasts of the birds; top each with 2 or 3 sprigs of sage. Wrap each bird with sliced prosciutto; tie with cotton string.

2 Meanwhile, in a large roasting pan, spread out the lentils. Top with the leek, apricots, 2 more sage sprigs, 2 thyme sprigs, and garlic. Set the pheasants or hens on top and pour the cider over. Roast the birds and lentils, uncovered, for 45 minutes.

3 Meanwhile, in a small saucepan, bring the 1½ cups chicken stock to a boil over high heat. Pour the stock over the pheasants or hens and cover the birds (not the lentils) with foil. Return to the oven and roast 45 minutes more for the pheasant (only 30 minutes more for the Cornish hens) or until the juices of the birds run clear when a thigh is pierced with a fork.

4 Transfer the birds to a platter and keep warm. Stir the lentil mixture, adding another ½ cup of boiling chicken stock to the roasting pan if the lentils seem dry. Return the lentils to the oven to cook, uncovered, for another 15 minutes or until tender.

5 Spoon the lentils around the birds. Decorate with additional sage and thyme sprigs, and the orange wedges.

More ideas

• Cover each pheasant with strips of turkey bacon instead of prosciutto.

• Pheasants with orange wild rice: Stuff the birds as directed in step 1 and place in a roasting pan. Omit the lentil mixture (step 2). Pour the cider over the birds and roast as in steps 2 and 3. While the birds are roasting, prepare 2 packages (10 ounces each) of wild-rice mix, according to the package directions, adding 1 tablespoon of orange zest to the cooking water. Coarsely chop 2 cups of fresh orange sections and toss with the cooked rice. Surround the birds with the rice (step 5).

Healthy tips

• Lentils are an excellent source of fiber, folate, and iron. They also provide good amounts of many minerals such as copper, potassium, magnesium, and zinc.

• Dried apricots provide excellent amounts of beta-carotene, which the body converts into vitamin A, plus potassium and soluble fiber. In addition, dried apricots are especially valuable for vegetarians as a good source of iron and copper.

main course poultry

Chinese barbecued duck

Long Island, New York is known for producing some of the finest, full-breasted ducks, famous for their dark juicy rich meat. To barbecue, first trim the duck of any visible fat, then prick the skin and fat, but not the meat. As the duck grills, excess fat under the skin drips away. For extra flavor, baste and glaze with a honey-soy sauce.

Makes 6 servings

Barbecued duck

1 duck (about 4½ pounds), giblets removed
3 tablespoons hoisin sauce
2 teaspoon dried thyme leaves
2 teaspoons five-spice powder
⅓ cup golden honey
¼ cup reduced-sodium soy sauce
2 large cloves garlic

Chinese snowpeas

1 tablespoon peanut oil
12 ounces snowpeas (3 cups)
1 large garlic clove, minced
½ cup drained canned bamboo shoots
1 tablespoon orange zest
½ cup fresh orange juice
1 tablespoon reduced-sodium soy sauce

Preparation time: 30 minutes
Marinating time: at least 1 hour
Grilling time: 30 minutes

Each serving (without skin) provides
calories 310, total fat 12g, saturated fat 4g, cholesterol 76mg, sodium 770mg, total carbohydrate 28g, dietary fiber 3g, protein 23g

✓✓✓	C
✓✓	B₂, niacin
✓	B₁, B₆, iron, potassium, zinc, copper, fiber

1 First, prepare the duck for grilling. Using a boning knife or poultry shears, cut along both sides of the backbone and lift it out (avoid cutting through the skin). Trim off as much fat as you can and cut off any extra flaps of skin. Place the bird on a flat surface, skin-side up, and press down firmly with the palm of your hand to flatten out the bird.

2 Using a metal skewer or meat fork, prick the duck all over, piercing through the skin and fat but not into the meat. In a cup, mix the hoisin sauce, thyme, and five-spice powder, and spread all over the duck. Weave 2 parallel skewers (at least 15 inches) through the bird to hold it flat, then spread it out, breast-side down, in a large shallow dish.

3 Now make the marinade. In a measuring cup, whisk together the honey, soy sauce, and garlic, then pour over the duck. Cover with plastic wrap and marinate in the refrigerator for at least 1 hour or overnight, turning the bird at least one time.

4 Now, barbecue the duck. Preheat the grill or broiler to medium-high. Lift the duck out of the marinade and transfer it to the grill rack or broiler pan, about 6 inches from the heat. In a small saucepan, bring the marinade

to a boil over high heat. Grill or broil the duck for 30 minutes (turning it once) or until the juices of the duck run clear when a thigh is pierced with a fork. During grilling, frequently baste the bird with the rest of the marinade. If the duck browns too quickly, line the rack with foil and continue cooking the bird directly on the foil.

5 Meanwhile, cook the snowpeas. In a large skillet, heat the oil over high heat. Add the snowpeas and garlic and stir-fry 2 minutes or just until the peas wilt. Stir in the bamboo shoots and stir-fry 1 minute more. Add the orange zest and juice and the soy sauce and stir-fry 2 minutes more or until heated through.

6 Transfer the duck to a carving board and carefully remove the skin. Place on a serving platter and spoon the vegetables around the bird.

Healthy tip

● Snowpeas provide good amounts of soluble fiber, which can help to lower high blood cholesterol levels. They are an excellent source of vitamin C: ½ cup serving provides 50% of the Daily Value.

● Duck, without the skin, is a good source of the B vitamins, of thiamine, riboflavin, niacin, and B₆.

More ideas

• Barbecued duck with brandied cranberry glaze: Omit the hoisin sauce (step 2) and the marinade (step 3). Instead, heat 1 can of jellied cranberry sauce (16 ounces), ⅓ cup of cranberry juice, and ¼ teaspoon of ground cinnamon in a small saucepan until the jelly melts completely. Remove from the heat and stir in 3 tablespoons of cherry brandy. Pour over the duck and proceed with marinating and grilling the duck (steps 3 and 4). Stir in 1 cup of dried cherries with the bamboo shoots (step 5).

• Barbecued duck breasts: If you would like barbecued duck without roasting a whole duck, substitute 2 pounds of boneless skinless duck breasts for the whole duck (steps 1 and 2). Do not prick the duck. For medium doneness, grill the duck breasts about 15 minutes (step 4).

Chicken Bourguignonne

In the French countryside, braised meats are traditionally simmered in robust red Burgundy wine, usually with mushrooms, onions, and bacon. For this healthier version, substitute chicken breasts for the whole chicken. You save on both fat and calories, without sacrificing flavor. Serve with sautéed new potatoes and French bread.

Makes 6 servings

2 pounds small white onions (about 16)

6 slices lean turkey bacon

3 tablespoons garlic-flavored olive oil

2 pounds boneless skinless chicken breasts

1 teaspoon *each* salt and black pepper

8 ounces white mushrooms

12 sprigs of parsley, 5 inches long

8 sprigs of fresh thyme, 5 inches long

1 large bay leaf

2 cups chicken stock, preferably homemade (see page 23), or low-sodium chicken broth

1½ cups full-bodied Burgundy red wine

2 cups bite-size peeled carrot chunks

1 teaspoon sugar

2 tablespoons cornstarch

¼ cup cold water

To decorate

½ cup minced fresh parsley

Preparation time: 30 minutes
Cooking time: about 1¼ hours

Each serving provides

calories 434, total fat 15g, saturated fat 3g, cholesterol 97mg, sodium 709mg, total carbohydrate 26g, dietary fiber 5g, protein 40g

✓✓✓	A, niacin, B$_6$
✓✓	C, potassium
✓	B$_1$, B$_2$, folate, calcium, iron, magnesium, zinc, copper, fiber

1 In a heatproof bowl, place the onions. Pour boiling water over to cover, let stand about 1 minute, transfer to a colander and cool under cold running water. Peel, cut any large ones in half lengthwise, and set aside.

2 Cut the bacon crosswise, on a slant, into thin strips, ¼ inch wide. In a 6-quart flameproof Dutch oven or casserole, heat 1 tablespoon of the oil over medium-high heat. Add the onions and bacon and stir for 5 minutes or until the onions are golden brown and the bacon is crispy. Using a slotted spoon, transfer the mixture to a platter lined with paper towels.

3 Cut the chicken breasts into fillets, about 4 inches by 3 inches and season with half of the salt and pepper. Drizzle 1 more tablespoon of the oil into the Dutch oven; add the chicken. Sauté for 7 minutes or until golden brown all over, turning each piece one time. Using the slotted spoon, transfer to the plate with the bacon and onions.

4 Wash the mushrooms and quarter them. Heat the remaining oil in the Dutch oven, add the mushrooms, and sprinkle with the rest of the salt and pepper. Sauté for 5 minutes or until golden brown.

5 Return the chicken, onions, and bacon to the Dutch oven with the mushrooms and stir to distribute the ingredients. Add the parsley, thyme, and bay leaf. Pour in the stock and wine.

6 Increase the heat to high, bring to a boil, and add the carrots. Lower the heat to medium-low, cover, and simmer for 35 minutes or until the carrots are tender and the juices of the chicken run clear when a breast is pierced with a fork. Discard the bay leaf. Using a slotted spoon, arrange all of the ingredients on a serving platter.

7 Increase the heat to high, add the sugar to the pan juices, and boil, uncovered, until reduced to about 2 cups. In a cup, dissolve the cornstarch in the water; whisk into the pan juices. Return to a boil and cook for 2 minutes or until the gravy thickens. Spoon the sauce over the chicken and vegetables and sprinkle with the parsley.

Healthy tip

• Cooking decreases the nutritional value of most vegetables — but not of carrots. Raw carrots have tough cell walls. But, cooking them breaks down the cell membranes, making it even easier for the body to absorb the beta-carotene, which the body converts to vitamin A.

main course poultry

More ideas

• Chicken Riesling: Turn this recipe into a dish that is typical of the Alsace region of north-eastern France. For the 2 pounds of boneless skinless chicken, use half breasts and half thighs. Cut into servings pieces (step 3).

Substitute 1½ cups of Riesling white wine for the Burgundy (step 5). Add 2 cups of frozen peas (use the small petite peas if you can find them) during the last 5 minutes of cooking (step 6). After thickening the pan juices (step 7), stir in ¼ cup of heavy cream and

heat through (do not boil). Serve over cooked wide egg noodles tossed with poppy seeds.

• If you cannot find garlic-flavored olive oil, substitute extra virgin olive oil and sauté 2 large minced garlic cloves with the mushrooms (steps 2, 3, and 4).

Chicken Marsala with fennel

From the Sicilian city of Marsala comes this famous fortified wine with a deep amber color. Choose the dry superiore type for this dish. Begin with your favorite parts of the chicken, then sauté with leeks, fennel, green peas, and Marsala. Another day, try substituting tomatoes and red bell peppers for the fennel.

Makes 6 servings

4 pounds chicken parts on the bone (breasts, legs, and thighs)

¼ cup all-purpose flour

¾ teaspoon freshly ground black pepper

½ teaspoon salt

2 tablespoons extra virgin olive oil

1 large leek or 2 extra large yellow onions, sliced (3 cups)

2 tablespoons slivered basil leaves

1 teaspoon fennel seeds

⅔ cup dry Marsala wine

2 cups chicken stock, preferably homemade (see page 23), or low-sodium chicken broth

2 large fennel bulbs (1 pound), trimmed and cut into bite-size chunks (3 cups)

2 cups fresh or frozen peas

1 large lemon

1 tablespoon cornstarch

⅓ cup finely chopped parsley

Preparation time: 30 minutes
Cooking time: 1 hour

Each serving (without skin) provides

calories 390, total fat 13g, saturated fat 3g, cholesterol 96mg, sodium 472mg, total carbohydrate 27g, dietary fiber 3g, protein 37g

✓✓✓	niacin, C
✓✓	B_6
✓✓	B_1, B_2, folate, calcium, iron, magnesium, potassium, zinc, copper, fiber

1 Remove the skin from the chicken. Shake the flour and half of the pepper and salt in a self-sealing plastic bag. Add the chicken, a few pieces at a time, seal, and shake until well coated.

2 In a large skillet or sauté pan, heat 1 tablespoon of the oil over medium-high heat. Add the leek, basil, and fennel seeds and sauté for 5 minutes or until the leek softens. Using a slotted spoon, transfer the leek mixture to a large plate and set aside.

3 Add the remaining oil to the skillet and sauté the chicken for 7 minutes or until golden brown all over. Transfer the chicken to the plate with the leek mixture and keep warm.

4 Pour ⅓ cup of the Marsala into the hot skillet and let it simmer until it reduces to about half. Stir in the stock and bring to a simmer. Return the leek mixture and pieces of dark chicken meat to the skillet (wait to add the breasts, as they can overcook). Stir in the fennel.

5 Reduce the heat to medium-low, cover, and simmer the chicken mixture for 15 minutes. Add the chicken breasts, cover, and simmer 10 minutes more. Then stir in the peas and continue to cook 5 minutes more or until the juices of the chicken run clear when a thigh is pierced with a fork. Using

a slotted spoon, transfer the chicken and the vegetables to a serving platter and keep warm.

6 Remove several strips of lemon zest from the lemon and set aside. Squeeze the juice into the skillet. In a cup, dissolve the cornstarch in the remaining ⅓ cup of Marsala, whisk into the pan juices, and boil for 2 minutes or until the sauce thickens. Spoon the sauce over the chicken and vegetables. Sprinkle with the lemon zest and parsley and serve immediately.

main course poultry

More ideas
- Chicken Italiano: Sauté 2 cups of red bell pepper strips, ¼ inch thick, with the leek and basil; omit the fennel seeds (step 2). Add 2 cups of tomato wedges with the peas (step 5). Substitute ½ cup of additional slivered basil leaves for the parsley (step 6).
- Chicken Marsala with fresh asparagus: Substitute 2 cups of fresh asparagus tips for the peas (step 5).
- White chicken meat Marsala: Substitute 1½ pounds of boneless skinless chicken breast fillets for the chicken parts (step 1). Cook the breasts for only 10 minutes, then add the peas and cook 5 minutes more (step 5).

Pheasant casserole with wine

Look for farm-raised pheasants in specialty meat markets. They are generally more tender, juicier, and milder in flavor than the wild variety. Cut up the birds, brown in a little hot oil, then cook in a covered casserole in wine and chicken stock. If you can not find pheasant, Cornish game hens work well in this recipe, too.

Makes 6 servings

2 pheasants, dressed (about 2¼ pounds each), or 6 Cornish game hens (about 1¼ to 1½ pounds each), giblets removed

1 pound white onions, peeled and halved (2 cups)

1 large fennel bulb (about 12 ounces)

6 slices turkey bacon

2 tablespoons sunflower oil

2 large cloves garlic, minced

½ teaspoon freshly ground black pepper

1⅓ cups dry white wine, such as white Burgundy

1⅓ cups chicken stock, preferably homemade (see page 23), or low-sodium chicken broth

Preparation time: 30 minutes
Cooking time: about 1¼ hours

Each serving provides

calories 437, total fat 22g, saturated fat 6g, cholesterol 116mg, sodium 360mg, total carbohydrate 12g, dietary fiber 1g, protein 40g

✓✓✓	niacin, B$_6$
✓✓	C
✓	B$_1$, B$_2$, iron, magnesium, potassium, zinc, copper

1 Preheat the oven to 375°F. Cut the pheasants or the hens into 8 serving pieces each. Peel and halve the onions. Trim the fennel (save any feathery leaves for decorating). Cut the bulb lengthwise into 8 wedges. Cut the bacon into strips, 1 inch wide.

2 In a 12-cup Dutch oven or 3-quart rangetop and ovenproof casserole, heat the oil over medium-high heat. Add the birds, onions, bacon, and garlic and sauté until the birds are golden-brown on all sides and the bacon begins to cook. Stir in the wedges of fennel and the pepper.

3 Pour in the wine and then add the chicken stock. The liquid should come halfway up the vegetables and meat, but not cover them. If necessary, add a little more stock. Bring the liquid to a boil and remove from the heat.

4 Cover the Dutch oven or casserole and transfer to the oven. Cook for 1 to 1¼ hours or until the birds are tender and the juices of the birds run clear when a thigh is pierced with a fork. Sprinkle with the reserved fennel leaves and serve immediately.

Healthy tip

• Pheasant is an excellent source of protein and the B vitamins niacin and B$_6$. Niacin is needed for energy metabolism and keeping the skin, as well as the nervous and digestive systems, healthy. B$_6$ is needed to help make red blood cells.

More ideas

• Country-style pheasant with mushrooms: Omit the fennel (steps 1 and 2). At the beginning of step 2 and before sautéing the birds, heat 1 tablespoon of unsalted butter in the Dutch oven, add 3 cups of sliced white mushrooms, cut ¼ inch thick, and sauté until golden; transfer to a plate. Proceed with step 2. Return the mushrooms to the Dutch oven with the fennel (end of step 2). Substitute 1⅓ cups red Burgundy wine for the white wine.

• Duckling with mushrooms: Prepare as for Country-style pheasant (above), substituting 6 pounds of duck pieces, cut up, for the pheasant (steps 1 and 2). Stir in ¼ cup of orange marmalade at the end of step 2.

Chicken and sausage jambalaya

The name of the famous Cajun-Creole dish probably comes from the French jambon *(ham), which often appeared in the early jambalayas in the late 19th century. Here it teams up with chicken and traditional flavors.*

Makes 8 servings

1 pound chorizo sausage (2 cups)
12 ounces cooked smoked ham (1½ cups)
1½ pounds boneless skinless chicken breasts
4 teaspoons Cajun seasoning (see right)
2 extra-large yellow onions (3 cups)
2 large green bell peppers (2 cups)
3 ribs celery (1½ cups)
2 tablespoons sunflower oil
2 large garlic cloves, minced
3 tablespoons all-purpose flour
1 tablespoon chopped fresh sage leaves
1 tablespoon chopped fresh thyme leaves
2 large bay leaves
2 cups uncooked long-grain white rice
3½ cups chicken stock, preferably homemade
  (see page 23), or low-sodium chicken broth
1 can whole tomatoes in juice (14½ ounces)
Hot pepper sauce (such as Tabasco) to taste
6 green onions, trimmed and sliced
½ cup chopped parsley

Preparation time: 30 minutes
Cooking time: 50 minutes

Each serving provides

calories 432, **total fat** 25g, **saturated fat** 8g, **cholesterol** 85mg, **sodium** 579mg, **total carbohydrate** 51g, **dietary fiber** 3g, **protein** 48g

✓✓✓	niacin, C
✓✓	B₁, B₆
✓	A, B₂, iron, magnesium, potassium, zinc, copper

1 Slice the chorizo ¼ inch thick and dice the ham. Cut the chicken into bite-size pieces and coat all sides of the chicken with 2 teaspoons of the Cajun seasoning. Coarsely chop the yellow onions. Remove the stems, membranes, and seeds from the bell peppers and coarsely chop them. Thinly slice the celery.

2 In a 6-quart Dutch oven or saucepot, heat 1 tablespoon of the oil over medium-high heat. Add the chorizo and ham and sauté for 3 minutes. Add the chicken and sauté 5 minutes more or until the chicken is brown on all sides. Using a slotted spoon, transfer the mixture to a plate and keep warm.

3 Add the remaining oil to the hot Dutch oven. Stir in the onions, peppers, celery, and garlic and sauté 5 minutes or until the vegetables soften. Stir in the flour, sage, thyme, bay leaves, and the remaining Cajun seasoning; cook and stir constantly for 5 minutes or until the flour browns. Add the rice and sauté 2 minutes more. Return the chicken mixture, and any juices that have collected, to the pan.

4 Pour in the stock plus the tomatoes and their juice; stir well to break up the tomatoes. Bring to a full boil. Lower the heat to medium-low, cover, and simmer for 20 minutes or until the rice

has absorbed almost all the liquid. Discard the bay leaves and season to taste with the hot pepper sauce. Top with the green onions and parsley.

More ideas

• If you cannot find chorizo sausage, choose any other spicy smoked pork sausage.

• If your grocer does not have ready-made Cajun seasoning, use a mixture of 1 tablespoon of paprika and 1 teaspoon of cayenne pepper.

• Bayou jambalaya: Omit the chorizo sausage (steps 1 and 2). At the beginning, shell and devein 1½ pounds large shrimp; cook in boiling water for 3 minutes or just until they turn opaque. Transfer the shrimp to a colander and rinse with cold water; set aside. Add the shrimp to the jambalaya during the last 5 minutes of cooking (step 4).

Healthy tips

• Green pepper provides vitamin C and beta-carotene, both of which have strong protective antioxidant functions against cancer, heart disease, and stroke.

• Even when used in moderation, sunflower oil provides good amounts of vitamin E. This vitamin helps prevent the oxidation of vitamin A and fats. It also helps to maintain healthy red blood cells and muscle tissue and protects the lungs against pollutants.

Chicken and potato curry

Recipes abound for this traditional spicy East Indian stew. The secret to this recipe is marinating the chicken, without its skin, with a ginger-lemony mixture for half an hour — just enough time to soak in all of the flavor. If you wish, this curry is even more special if you serve it with side dishes of chutney and toasted coconut.

Makes 6 servings

4 pounds chicken parts on the bone
  (breasts, legs, and thighs)
2 tablespoons fresh lemon juice
1 tablespoon peeled chopped gingerroot
½ teaspoon ground turmeric
½ teaspoon salt
2 tablespoons sunflower oil
2 tablespoons all-purpose flour
2 teaspoons curry powder, or to taste
½ dried small red chili (discard seeds)
¼ teaspoon ground cumin
2 large yellow onions, slivered (2 cups)
1 large green bell pepper, seeded and
  thinly sliced (1 cup)
3 large garlic cloves, minced
1 can whole tomatoes in juice (14½ ounces)
¾ cup chicken stock, preferably homemade
  (see page 23), or low-sodium chicken broth
1 pound all-purpose potatoes, peeled
2 cups shredded green cabbage
  (about 5 ounces)
2 cups frozen peas (one 10-ounce package),
  thawed

Preparation time: 30 minutes
Marinating time: 30 minutes
Cooking time: 50 minutes

1 Remove the skin from the chicken. Place in a single layer in a large shallow baking dish. Using a sharp pointed knife, cut 3 slashes in each piece, right to the bone. In a cup, mix the lemon juice, gingerroot, turmeric, and salt; rub all over the chicken. Refrigerate for 30 minutes.

2 In a large skillet, heat the oil over medium-high heat. Stir in the flour, curry powder (add a little more if you wish), dried chili, and cumin. Cook for 1 minute. Stir in the onions, bell pepper, and garlic; sauté 5 minutes or until the vegetables soften. Stir in the chicken, tomatoes and their juice, and the stock. Reduce the heat to medium-low, cover, and cook for 15 minutes.

3 Meanwhile, half-fill a large saucepan with water and bring to a boil over high heat. Cut the potatoes into bite-size chunks (you need 2 cups) and boil for 5 minutes. Drain well.

4 Stir the potatoes and cabbage into the curried chicken mixture. Cover the pan again and continue to simmer 20 minutes more or until the juices of the chicken run clear when a thigh is pierced with a fork. Add the peas and cook 5 minutes more. Serve the curry hot, with pita bread.

Healthy tips

- The humble potato is an excellent source of vitamin C, the vitamin known for promoting healing of wounds. This vitamin strengthens the blood vessel walls, as well as maintains collagen, the connective tissue that holds the cells of the body together.
- The vitamin C provided by the peppers, tomatoes, and potatoes increases the absorption of iron from the chicken.
- All the water-soluble vitamins from the vegetables — such as vitamin C from the peas, tomatoes, and potatoes and the B vitamins from the peas — are retained in the sauce of this curry. This dish is not only good, but good for you. So use some bread to sop up the sauce!

Each serving (without skin) provides
calories 416, total fat 13g, saturated fat 3g, cholesterol 96mg, sodium 473mg, total carbohydrate 36g, dietary fiber 6g, protein 38g

✓✓✓	niacin, C
✓✓	B₁, B₆, potassium
✓	A, B₂, folate, iron, magnesium, zinc, copper, fiber

More ideas

• Make-ahead tip: The flavor in this dish is even better if you make the recipe the day before you serve it. Why? The curry intensifies in flavor when the spices have had longer to soak into the all of the ingredients in the dish, especially the potatoes.

• Fresh fruit and chicken curry: Prepare the curry through step 2, increasing the flour to 3 tablespoons. Cook the chicken mixture for 30 minutes, not just 15 minutes (step 2). Omit the potatoes, cabbage, and peas (steps 3 and 4). Instead, add 2 cups of fresh pineapple chunks, 2 cups of fresh orange sections, and

1 cup of golden raisins to the curried chicken and continue to simmer, covered, 10 minutes more or until heated through. Serve the curry over steamed white rice tossed with a little ground nutmeg. For accompaniments, serve mango chutney, toasted coconut, and toasted slivered almonds.

Turkey mole

Coming from the word molli *(concoction), this spicy Mexican sauce is a rich blend of onions, garlic, and chili peppers. Traditionally, mole is made with Mexican chocolate, but in America, it's bitter chocolate. Stir in cooked turkey, raisins, and almonds, serve over steamed long-grain rice, and you have a delicious supper.*

Makes 4 servings

2 tablespoons sunflower oil

2 large yellow onions, chopped (2 cups)

2 large garlic cloves, minced

1½ tablespoons chili powder, or more to taste

1 tablespoon sesame seeds

1 small red chili pepper, seeded and minced

1½ pounds boneless skinless turkey breast
   steaks, cut into ½-inch-wide strips

½ teaspoon salt

1 can whole tomatoes in juice (14½ ounces)

⅔ cup dark raisins

½ teaspoon ground cloves

1 cup chicken stock, preferably homemade
   (see page 23), or low-sodium chicken broth

3 tablespoons chopped bittersweet chocolate

¼ cup toasted sliced almonds

2 tablespoons chopped fresh coriander

To decorate

Sprigs of fresh coriander

Preparation time: 30 minutes

Cooking time: 30 minutes

Each serving provides

calories 506, total fat 20g, saturated fat 5g,
cholesterol 118mg, sodium 612mg, total
carbohydrate 39g, dietary fiber 7g, protein 50g

✓✓✓	niacin, B$_6$, C
✓✓	iron, magnesium, potassium, copper, fiber
✓	A, B$_1$, B$_2$, folate, calcium, zinc

1 In a large skillet, heat the oil over medium-high heat. Add the onions, garlic, chili powder, sesame seeds, and chili pepper. Sauté for 10 minutes or until the onions are soft and the sesame seeds are fragrant and toasted.

2 Season the strips of turkey with the salt. Add the turkey to the skillet and toss with the onion mixture. Stir in the canned tomatoes with their juice and the raisins. Sprinkle in the cloves.

3 Pour in the stock and bring to a full boil. Reduce the heat to medium-low, cover the skillet, and simmer gently for 10 minutes.

4 Add the chocolate, almonds and chopped coriander, and stir until the chocolate has melted. Spoon into a serving dish and decorate with sprigs of coriander.

More ideas

• Turkey mole tacos: At end of step 3, dissolve 2 teaspoons of cornstarch dissolved in ¼ cup of cold water, then whisk into the turkey mixture. Bring to a boil and cook for2 minutes or until the sauce thickens. Then add the chocolate, almonds, and coriander, and stir until the chocolate melts and the sauce bubbles and thickens (step 4). Preheat the oven to 350°F. Now, make a salad: Toss 4 cups of shredded leaf or iceberg lettuce, 1 cup of thin avocado slices, 1 cup of slivered yellow onions, 1 cup of chopped tomatoes, and ¼ cup of fresh coriander leaves. Place 12 crisp taco shells (the folded ones) directly on the oven rack and heat for 3 minutes. To make the tacos, stuff each taco shell about half full with ⅓ cup to ½ cup of the mole mixture. Spoon the salad on top of the mole mixture until it almost overflows. Eat right away, as the shells may become soggy upon standing.

• Quick mole: Omit the uncooked turkey breast steaks and the salt (step 2). Instead, stir 3 cups of cooked bite-size pieces of turkey into the onion mixture and proceed with the addition of the tomatoes and the rest of the ingredients. Simmer gently for 7 minutes, not 10 (step 3).

Healthy tips

• Research has shown that lycopene – the natural pigment which gives tomatoes their red color – can reduce the risk of heart disease and prostate cancer. A 6-year study of 48,000 men, conducted at Harvard Medical School, found that those consuming tomato products at least four times a week had a 20% lower risk of prostate cancer than those not eating tomatoes. Processed tomatoes, such as canned tomatoes and tomato paste, contain much higher concentrations of lycopene than fresh.

• Raisins are a good source for potassium and a fair source of iron and fiber.

Chicken and rosemary cobbler

Here's a deep-dish savory pie that uses the ingredients from a Sicilian kitchen, many flavors found in the Italian countryside, and a cobbler technique from grandmother's day. The filling combines succulent chunks of chicken, sweet green peppers, fresh mushrooms, and olives in a tomato sauce. Wedges of rosemary biscuits top it off.

Makes 8 servings

4 pounds chicken pieces on the bone
  (breasts, legs, thighs)
2 sprigs of fresh rosemary, 5 inches long
1 large bay leaf
2 large yellow onions (2 cups)
2 large green bell peppers (3 cups)
6 ounces mushrooms (2 cups)
2 tablespoons sunflower oil
2 large garlic cloves, minced
1 can chopped tomatoes in juice (28-ounces)
2 tablespoons medium-dry sherry
1 cup pitted black olives

Rosemary biscuit topping

2 cups self-rising white flour
1 teaspoon baking powder
1 teaspoon chopped fresh rosemary leaves
¾ teaspoon freshly ground black pepper
½ cup (1 stick) unsalted butter
⅔ cup low-fat milk (2% milkfat)

Preparation time: 30 minutes
Cooking time: about 1¼ hours

Each serving (without skin) provides

calories 410, **total fat** 23g, **saturated fat** 9g, **cholesterol** 68mg, **sodium** 924mg, **total carbohydrate** 36g, **dietary fiber** 3g, **protein** 18g

✓✓✓	C
✓✓	niacin, calcium
✓	A, B$_1$, B$_2$, B$_6$, iron, copper, fiber

1 First, cook the chicken pieces (leave on the bone). In an 8-quart saucepot, place the chicken, rosemary sprigs, and bay leaf. Cover with water and bring to a boil over high heat. Lower the heat to medium-low and simmer for 45 minutes or until the chicken is tender and almost falling off the bones.

2 While the chicken cooks, prepare the vegetables. Cut the onions into thin slivers. Remove the stems and seeds from the bell peppers, then slice into thin slivers . Wash and quarter the mushrooms.

3 Using a slotted spoon, transfer the chicken to a cutting board. When it is cool enough to handle, remove the meat from the bones. Discard the skin and cut the meat into bite-size chunks.

4 In a large sauté pan or saucepan, heat the oil over medium-high heat. Add the onions, peppers, mushrooms, and garlic; sauté for 5 minutes or until the onions start to brown. Stir in the canned tomatoes with their juice, the sherry, and olives. Taste and season with a little black pepper, if you wish. Remove from the heat; set aside in pan.

5 Preheat the oven to 425°F and butter a deep 9-inch round or square baking dish (2-quart capacity). Now, make the biscuit topping. In a medium-size bowl, mix the flour, baking powder, rosemary, and pepper. Cut in 6 tablespoons (¾ of a stick) of the butter until the mixture resembles fine crumbs. Make a well in the center and pour in the milk. Mix just until a soft, slightly sticky dough forms, adding a little more milk if necessary.

6 Stir the cooked chicken into the vegetable mixture in the saucepan. Bring to a simmer and cook 3 minutes more or until hot. Spoon into the baking dish and spread the biscuit dough on top. Melt the rest of the butter and drizzle over the dough. Bake for 12 minutes or until the biscuit topping is puffed and golden brown. Serve hot.

Healthy tips

• When buying flour, look for an all-purpose enriched variety. It is not only an excellent source of starch, but also a good source of iron, and the B vitamins of thiamine, riboflavin, niacin, and folate. It provides dietary fiber, particularly the insoluble variety.
• Peppers are packed with vitamin C; ounce for ounce they offer 40% more vitamin C than oranges. They are also rich in beta-carotene, which the body converts into vitamin A.

More ideas

- Chicken cobbler olé: To cook the chicken, substitute 2 large cloves of garlic for the rosemary and bay leaf (step 1). Add 1 large red bell pepper with the 2 green bell peppers; omit the mushrooms and sherry (steps 3 and 4). Cook 2 teaspoons of chili powder and 2 teaspoons of cumin with the onion mixture (step 4). Substitute a corn-bread topping for the biscuit topping (steps 5 and 6): Use two 8½-ounce packages of corn-bread mix and prepare according to package directions. Spread the batter on top of the cobbler. Sprinkle the top with ⅓ cup of shredded Cheddar cheese. Bake the cobbler at 400°F, uncovered, for 15 minutes or until the corn-bread topping is golden brown and a pick inserted in the center comes out with a moist crumb.

- For variety, add 2 cups bite-size, parboiled peeled carrots with the tomatoes; substitute 2 tablespoons Madeira wine for sherry (step 4).

Turkey drumsticks braised with baby vegetables

In the typical French manner of braising foods, brown turkey drumsticks in hot oil, then slowly oven-roast them in an herb-seasoned stock. Add a medley of baby vegetables during the last 30 minutes. Or, try this recipe with a whole turkey breast instead; just double the vegetables and serve eight guests, instead of four.

Makes 4 servings

Turkey drumsticks

2 large turkey drumsticks on the bone (about 1½ pounds each)

¾ teaspoon freshly ground black pepper

½ teaspoon salt

2 tablespoons sunflower oil

1½ cups turkey stock, preferably homemade (see page 23), or low-sodium chicken broth

2 sprigs *each* fresh rosemary and thyme

1 bay leaf

Baby vegetables

2 pounds yellow onions, sliced ¼ inch thick

2 cups baby zucchini, trimmed

2 cups peeled baby carrots

2 cups drained canned baby corn

Preparation time: 15 minutes

Cooking time: 1½ hours

Each serving (without skin) provides

calories 488, total fat 18g, saturated fat 4g, cholesterol 109mg, sodium 544mg, total carbohydrate 47g, dietary fiber 9g, protein 38g

✓✓✓	A, B₆
✓✓	B₂, niacin, folate, C, potassium, zinc, copper, fiber
✓	B₁, calcium, iron, magnesium

1 First, preheat the oven to 350°F. Season the turkey drumsticks all over with the pepper and salt. In a large flameproof Dutch oven, heat the oil over a medium-high heat. Add the drumsticks and fry until brown, turning them frequently. Pour the stock over the drumsticks; add the rosemary and thyme sprigs, and the bay leaf.

2 Cover the Dutch oven and transfer the drumsticks to the oven; cook, covered, for 1 hour.

3 Sprinkle the vegetables around the drumsticks and continue to cook, still covered, for 30 minutes more or until the vegetables are tender. When ready to serve, the turkey will be golden brown and the juices of the drumsticks will run clear when pierced with a fork; the vegetables should be tender, but not overcooked. Discard the bay leaf.

4 To serve, slice the meat off of the turkey drumsticks and serve with the vegetables. Drizzle a little of the pan juices over both the meat and the vegetables.

More ideas

● Braised chicken drumsticks: Substitute 8 chicken drumsticks (a total of 2 pounds) for the turkey drumsticks (step 1). Continue with step 2, roasting for only 30 minutes, instead of 1 hour, before adding the vegetables (step 3).

● Roasted turkey breast: Substitute 1 whole turkey breast, on the bone (about 5 pounds), for the turkey drumsticks (step 1). Continue with step 2, roasting the turkey breast for 1½ hours, instead of 1 hour, before adding *double* the amount of vegetables. If you wish, use chunks of peeled carrots and zucchini instead of the baby ones. Makes 8 servings

● Substitute 1½ cups of dry white wine for the turkey stock.

Healthy tips

● The beta-carotene found in carrots, which the body converts into vitamin A, is better absorbed by the body if the carrots have been cooked. Antioxidants, such as beta-carotene and Vitamin C, are essential to the diet, because they help protect against certain kinds of cancer.

● The sweet corn in this recipe also provides some vitamin A (from beta-carotene), as well as fiber.

Barbecued jerk chicken

Barbecuing (grilling foods over dry heat) is one of the oldest methods of cooking. Here, chicken is coated with a fiery hot jerk rub, typical of the spice rubs used in the Caribbean isles. For even more flavor, "mop" the chicken with a barbecue sauce — an all-American tomato one, a hickory-smoked Texas one, or a Carolina vinegary one.

Makes 4 servings

8 chicken drumsticks or thighs on the bone
(2 pounds)

Jamaican jerk rub

3 tablespoons extra virgin olive oil

½ cup minced green onions

3 large garlic cloves, minced

1 fresh red chili, minced (seeds removed)

1 Scotch Bonnet chili pepper, minced
(seeds removed)

3 sprigs fresh thyme leaves (5 inches)

½ teaspoon ground allspice

½ teaspoon salt

½ teaspoon freshly ground black pepper

½ cup bottled jerk sauce

To decorate

Lime wedges

Preparation time: 20 minutes
Marinating time: at least 1 hour
Grilling or broiling time: 25 minutes

Each serving (without skin) provides

calories 325, total fat 15g, saturated fat 3g, cholesterol 82mg, sodium 553mg, total carbohydrate 21g, dietary fiber 1g, protein 25g

✓✓✓	C
✓✓	niacin
✓	B_2, B_6, iron, zinc

1 First, prepare the chicken. Make a few shallow slashes, each about 1 inch long, in every piece, then place in a single layer in a shallow dish.

2 Now, make the jerk rub. In a medium-size bowl, stir together all of the ingredients for the rub except the jerk sauce until blended and a thick paste forms. Stir in the jerk sauce.

3 Using your fingers, coat both sides of the chicken with the jerk rub mixture, rubbing it into the slashes in the meat. Cover with plastic wrap, refrigerate, and let marinate for 1 hour or overnight.

4 Preheat the grill or broiler to high. Now, cook the chicken. In a small saucepan, bring the jerk rub to a boil over high heat. Place the chicken on a rack about 6 inches from the heat. Depending on the thickness of the pieces, cook for 25 minutes or until the juices of the chicken run clear when a drumstick or thigh is pierced with a fork. Baste frequently with the jerk rub, turning the chicken once.

5 Serve the chicken hot off the grill, decorated with the wedges of lime. Remove the skin from the chicken before serving.

More ideas

• All-American barbecue: Prepare rub, omitting the allspice and jerk sauce (step 2). While grilling (step 4), baste with All-American sauce: Whisk together 3 cups of bottled tomato ketchup, ½ cup *each* of cider vinegar, packed light brown sugar, and molasses, plus 3 tablespoons of Worcestershire sauce.

• Texas barbecue: Prepare rub, omitting the allspice and jerk sauce (step 2). While grilling (step 4), baste with Texas sauce: Whisk together 2 cups *each* of bottled tomato ketchup and chili sauce, ½ cup of cider vinegar, ⅓ cup of Worcestershire sauce, 2 tablespoons *each* of chili powder and liquid smoke, plus hot pepper sauce to taste.

• Carolina barbecue: Prepare rub, omitting the allspice and jerk sauce (step 2). While grilling (step 4), baste with Carolina sauce: Whisk together 1½ cups of cider vinegar, ½ cup of water, 1½ tablespoons of crushed hot pepper flakes, and 1 tablespoon of dry mustard.

Healthy tip

• The Mediterranean diet is thought to be much healthier than the average American diet. One reason? It uses olive oil, a monounsaturated fat, rather than butter and other saturated fats.

Teriyaki grilled Cornish hens

A hybrid bird of the Cornish and White Rock chickens, Rock Cornish (game) hens are small enough for every person to get a whole hen, tender enough to melt in your mouth, and thin enough when split open and flattened to grill quickly. Baste them with a Japanese-style marinade made from fresh gingerroot, soy sauce, and honey.

Serves 2

2 Rock Cornish hens (about 1½ pounds each)

Teriyaki baste

2 tablespoons toasted sesame oil

2 tablespoons reduced-sodium soy sauce

2 large garlic cloves, minced

1 tablespoon finely grated fresh gingerroot

1 tablespoon golden honey

½ teaspoon minced fresh red chili pepper
 (seeds and membranes discarded)

To decorate

2 whole long red chili peppers

To serve

Steamed jasmine rice or cooked
 angel hair pasta

Preparation time: 15 minutes

Marinating time: at least 30 minutes

Grilling or broiling time: 22 minutes

Each hen (without skin) provides

calories 445, total fat 22g, saturated fat 4g, cholesterol 217mg, sodium 693mg, total carbohydrate 12g, dietary fiber 0g, protein 49g

✓✓✓	niacin
✓✓	B₂, B₆
✓	B₁, B₁₂, E, iron, magnesium, potassium, zinc

1 First, prepare the hens. Using a boning knife or poultry shears, cut along both sides of the backbone of each hen and lift it out (avoid cutting though the skin). Place the hens on a flat surface, skin-side up, and press down firmly with the palm of your hand to flatten out the birds. Cut off the wing tips. Spread out the birds in a single layer in a large shallow dish.

2 Now, make the basting sauce. In a large measuring cup, whisk all of the ingredients for the teriyaki baste and pour over the hens. Cover with plastic wrap and marinate in the refrigerator for at least 30 minutes or overnight, turning the hens at least one time.

3 Meanwhile, make the chili peppers into "flowers." Holding each chili pepper by its stem-end, cut the peppers into long fine petals, three-fourths down the peppers. Soak in ice water for at least 30 minutes, so the petals fan apart.

4 Now, cook the hens. Preheat the grill or broiler to high. In a small saucepan, bring the teriyaki baste to a boil. Place the hens on a rack, skin-side down, about 6 inches from the heat. Cook for 22 minutes or until the juices of the hens run clear when a thigh is pierced with a fork. Baste frequently with the basting sauce, turning the hens once. If you wish, remove the skin.

Healthy tips

● Chili peppers contain capsaicin, which gives the peppers their fiery taste. Studies have shown that it also helps reduce nasal and sinus congestion. Additionally, chilies are cholesterol free and low in calories and sodium. They are also rich in beta carotene, which the body converts to vitamin A.

● Removing the skin from poultry reduces its fat content considerably. One 1½-pound Rock Cornish hen, cooked then served without the skin, contains 8.5 grams of fat, compared to 47 grams of fat for the same-size hen served with the skin.

More ideas

● Tomato-cumin baste: While making the basting sauce, omit the soy sauce, gingerroot, and minced chili pepper (step 2). To the sauce, add 2 tablespoons of bottled tomato ketchup, 1 tablespoon of Worcestershire sauce, 1 teaspoon of Dijon mustard, and ¼ teaspoon of cumin seeds.

● Japanese grilled chicken breasts: Substitute 4 boneless skinless chicken breasts (5 ounces each) for the hens. Grill for only 15 minutes.

● To serve 4 people, just double the recipe; to serve 6, triple the recipe.

main course poultry

106

Chicken *en goujon* with spicy dip

In France, en goujon *refers to small strips of fried fish, such as sole* en goujon. *Here, chicken breasts are cut into similar strips, and fried the healthier way — in the oven, not deep-fat-fried in a skillet. Serve with a spicy dip made with reduced-fat sour cream. And fry up a batch of potato fries or chips in the oven, the same low-fat way.*

Makes 6 servings

Spicy mustard dip

¾ cup reduced-fat sour cream

2 tablespoons whole-grain Dijon mustard

2 tablespoons snipped fresh chives

Chicken *en goujon*

1½ pounds boneless skinless chicken breasts

¼ teaspoon salt

1 teaspoon freshly ground black pepper

½ cup all-purpose flour

2 large eggs

2 tablespoons water

2 cups plain dry bread crumbs

¼ cup whole-grain Dijon mustard

1 large garlic clove, minced

1 tablespoon paprika

Preparation time: 30 minutes

Chilling time: 30 minutes

Cooking time: 15 minutes

Each serving provides

calories 394, **total fat 10g, saturated fat 2g,**
cholesterol 150mg, **sodium 981mg,** total
carbohydrate 38g, dietary fiber 1g, protein 35g

✓✓✓	niacin
✓✓	B₁, B₂, B₆
✓	A, calcium, iron, magnesium, potassium, zinc

1 First, make the spicy dip. Blend the sour cream, mustard, and chives. Spoon into a small serving bowl, cover with plastic wrap, and refrigerate.

2 Now, prepare the chicken. Cut the chicken lengthwise into strips, about 3 inches long and 1 inch wide, and sprinkle all over with all of the salt and half of the pepper.

3 In a self-sealing plastic bag, place the flour. In a pie plate, whisk the eggs and water until frothy. In a large shallow dish, mix the bread crumbs, mustard, garlic, paprika, and the rest of the pepper until blended.

4 Drop the chicken strips, a few at a time, into the bag of flour and shake until they are well coated. Shake off any excess flour. Dip the strips, first into the beaten eggs, then into the bread- crumb mixture, gently pressing the crumbs onto the chicken so they adhere. Arrange the strips on a large nonstick baking sheet and chill for 30 minutes.

5 Meanwhile, preheat the oven to 400°F. Bake the chicken strips for 15 minutes or until they are golden brown and crisp, turning once or twice. Serve hot or at room temperature with the chilled mustard dip.

More ideas

● Chicken *en goujon* Indienne: In the spicy dip, use only 1 tablespoon of whole-grain Dijon mustard (not 2) and stir in ½ teaspoon of curry powder (step 1). In the bread-crumb mixture, omit the mustard (step 3). Add 2 teaspoons of ground coriander, 1 teaspoon of ground cumin, ½ teaspoon of ground cardamom, and ½ teaspoon of ground cinnamon to the crumbs.

● Oven potato fries: Preheat the oven to 375°F. Peel 2 pounds of russet baking potatoes and cut into thick sticks, about 4 inches long and 1 inch thick. Soak in ice water for 15 minutes, then dry thoroughly on paper towels. Brush with 3 tablespoons of sunflower oil. Bake in a single layer on a nonstick baking sheet for 1 hour, turning 2 or 3 times. Toss with salt, if you wish.

● Oven potato chips: Follow directions for potato fries (above), except cut potatoes crosswise into thin slices, ⅛ inch thick. Bake at 400°F. for 35 minutes, tossing frequently.

Healthy tip

● Compared to other creams, reduced-fat sour cream is surprisingly low in fat and calories. One tablespoon of reduced-fat sour cream has 1 gram of fat and 20 calories, compared with 3 grams of fat and 30 calories for regular sour cream and 5½ grams of fat and 50 calories for heavy cream.

Turkey roulades

Look for some turkey breast steaks in your grocer's meat case. Pound them thin, then stuff them with fresh spinach leaves, roasted red peppers, ricotta cheese, and some freshly grated Parmesan. Braise them in stock and vermouth, then serve them with steamed fresh asparagus tips for an elegant dinner.

Makes 4 servings

Turkey roulades

4 boneless skinless turkey breast steaks
  (5 to 6 ounces each)

5 ounces fresh spinach leaves (3½ cups)

1 large red bell pepper, seeded and quartered

⅔ cup ricotta cheese

1 large egg, beaten

2 tablespoons freshly grated Parmesan
  cheese

2 tablespoons plain white bread crumbs

2 tablespoons chopped fresh basil leaves

⅛ teaspoon freshly grated or ground nutmeg

⅔ cup chicken stock, preferably homemade
  (see page 23), or low-sodium chicken broth

⅔ cup dry vermouth

⅓ cup reduced-fat sour cream

2 tablespoons light cream

Freshly ground black pepper

1 pound fresh asparagus spears, use tips only

Preparation time: 45 minutes
Cooking time: 35 minutes

Each serving provides

calories 437, **total fat 13g, saturated fat 6g,**
cholesterol 209mg, **sodium 298mg, total**
carbohydrate 14g, dietary fiber 1g, protein 56g

✓✓✓	A, niacin, B$_6$, folate, C
✓✓	B$_2$, calcium, iron, magnesium, potassium, zinc
✓	B$_1$, B$_{12}$, copper

1 First, prepare the roulades. Place each steak between 2 sheets of plastic wrap. Using a rolling pin, flatten into a 5-inch square, ¼ inch thick (don't worry if they are irregular in shape).

2 Wash the spinach, leaving some water on the leaves. Place in a large empty saucepan, cover, and cook over medium-high heat for 2 minutes or just until the leaves are wilted. Drain the spinach well, squeezing out any juices. Finely chop and put into a large bowl.

3 Preheat the grill or broiler. Place the red pepper, skin side up, on the rack and grill or broil for 6 minutes or until the skin is charred (do not turn over). Transfer the pepper to a paper bag and close tightly. Let stand (without peeking) until cool enough to handle, then discard the charred skin and dice.

4 Place the red pepper in the bowl with the spinach and mix with the ricotta cheese, beaten egg, Parmesan cheese (the freshly grated kind if possible), bread crumbs, basil, and nutmeg. Divide the filling among the turkey steaks, spreading it over them evenly. Roll up each turkey steak, folding over the sides to enclose the filling; close with wooden toothpicks.

5 In a large skillet, fit the roulades in a single layer and pour over the chicken stock and vermouth. Bring to a boil over high heat, then reduce the heat to medium-low, cover tightly, and simmer for 20 minutes. Using a slotted spoon, transfer the roulades to a plate and keep hot.

6 Increase the heat to high and boil the stock and vermouth mixture, uncovered, until reduced to ⅔ cup. Stir in the sour cream and light cream and cook 2 minutes more or until the sauce thickens. Add pepper to taste.

7 Meanwhile, cook asparagus tips in boiling water for 3 minutes or until just tender. Discard toothpicks from the roulades, then slice crosswise, 1 inch thick. Spoon sauce onto plates; arrange roulades and asparagus on top.

Healthy tips

● The ricotta and Parmesan cheeses are good sources of high-quality protein. And when used together, as in this recipe, they are a great way of adding flavor, as well as calcium, an essential nutrient for building strong bones and teeth.

● Asparagus is low in calories (6 spears have only 25 calories). It is an excellent source of folate, the vitamin that helps prevent neurological defects during pregnancy and may also help protect against heart disease.

Another idea

• Turkey roulades Italiano: Prepare the roulades as directed through step 4; omit roasting the red bell pepper. Omit the poaching sauce and asparagus. In a large skillet, heat 2 tablespoons of extra virgin olive oil over medium-high heat and brown the roulades all over. Transfer to a plate and keep hot. Add 1 cup *each* of red and yellow bell pepper strips (¼ inch wide),1 large red onion (cut into 6 wedges) and 6 peeled whole large garlic cloves. Sauté over medium-high heat for 5 minutes. Stir in 2 large plum tomatoes (cut each into 6 wedges), 12 large pitted black olives, and 1 tablespoon chopped fresh rosemary leaves. Arrange the roulades on top and pour over ½ cup dry white wine or chicken stock. Cover vegetables and simmer for 20 minutes, turning the roulades once. Remove the toothpicks and slice each roulade 1 inch thick. Spoon some of the sautéed vegetables on each plate and arrange the roulades on top.

Basil-stuffed chicken breasts

These stuffed chicken breasts look much more difficult to make than they really are — especially if you ask your butcher to cut the pockets in the chicken for you. Stuff with thin slices of mozzarella, fresh garden tomatoes, prosciutto, and plenty of fresh basil leaves. They're delicious served with tagliatelle (thin flat pasta noodles).

Makes 4 servings

Stuffed chicken breasts

4 boneless skinless chicken breast halves
   (5 ounces each)
½ teaspoon freshly ground black pepper
4 slices part-skim mozzarella cheese
   (1 ounce each)
1 large tomato, sliced ¼ inch thick
2 cups fresh basil leaves, 8 large leaves
   reserved, the remaining shredded
1 garlic clove, minced
4 slices prosciutto ham (½ ounce each)
1 tablespoon extra virgin olive oil

Gourmet salad

⅓ cup fresh lemon juice
2 tablespoons extra virgin olive oil
½ teaspoon *each* salt and black pepper
8 cups mesclun salad greens
2 cups watercress leaves

Preparation time: 1 hour
Cooking time: about 20 minutes

Each serving provides

calories 386, total fat 19g, saturated fat 6g,
cholesterol 107mg, sodium 656mg, total
carbohydrate 9g, dietary fiber 2g, protein 44g

✓✓✓	niacin, C
✓✓	A, B$_6$, calcium
✓	B$_1$, B$_2$, B$_{12}$, folate, iron, magnesium, potassium, zinc, copper

1 Preheat the oven to 425°F. Place each chicken breast on a flat surface. Make a lengthwise slit in each breast, about three-quarters of the way through, from one side toward the opposite one, to form a pocket.

2 Season the pockets of each chicken breast with a sprinkling of black pepper. Stuff each breast with 1 slice of cheese, 2 tomato slices, 2 tablespoons shredded basil, and some minced garlic.

3 Place 2 large basil leaves on top of each chicken breast, then wrap completely with a slice of prosciutto, making sure the ham covers the opening for the pocket. Tie each breast securely with 3 pieces of cotton kitchen string.

4 In a large skillet or a sauté pan (choose one with an ovenproof handle), heat the oil over medium-high heat. Add the chicken breasts and sauté for 5 minutes, turning to brown both sides. Transfer the pan to the oven. Bake for 12 minutes or until the juices of the chicken run clear when the thickest part of a breast is pierced with a fork.

5 Meanwhile, make the salad. In a large bowl, whisk the lemon juice, oil, salt, and pepper until the oil is suspended in the juice. Add the greens (such as arugula, frisée, mâche, oak leaf, radicchio) and watercress. Toss, then mound in the centers of 4 plates.

6 Discard the string from the chicken and slice crosswise, 1 inch thick (hold the roll together tightly while you cut). Place 1 sliced chicken breast on top of the salad on each of the 4 plates and decorate with the rest of the basil.

Another idea

• Feta-stuffed chicken breasts: Use 4 ounces of feta cheese instead of the mozzarella (step 2). For the shredded basil, substitute sautéed watercress (step 2). In a large skillet, melt 1 tablespoon of unsalted butter over medium-high heat. Add 2 cups of watercress leaves and cook for 1 minute or just until the watercress wilts. Season with ¼ teaspoon *each* of freshly ground black pepper and grated nutmeg.

Healthy tips

• Watercress is one of the most nutritious salad greens — plus it is low in calories and virtually fat free. It is a good source of the antioxidants in vitamin C and beta-carotene, which the body converts into vitamin A.

• Ounce for ounce, whole-milk mozzarella cheese contains 33% less fat and 30% fewer calories than Cheddar cheese. Part-skim mozzarella has 50% less fat and 36% fewer calories compared to the regular Cheddar cheese.

Turkey kebabs with fennel and red pepper relish

Marinate bites of turkey breast in white wine and fresh herbs. Then skewer with small onions and grill until golden brown. Serve with fennel and red pepper relish, and a generous helping of couscous or wild rice.

Makes 4 servings

Turkey kebabs

8 stalks of fresh rosemary or 8 wooden skewers

1 pound boneless skinless turkey breast steaks

½ teaspoon salt

½ teaspoon freshly ground black pepper

¼ cup dry white wine

3 tablespoons fresh lemon juice

2 large garlic cloves, minced

1 tablespoon chopped fresh rosemary leaves

1 tablespoon chopped fresh sage leaves

1 tablespoon fresh thyme leaves

1 teaspoon fennel seeds, lightly crushed

2 tablespoons extra virgin olive oil

16 small white onions, peeled

Red pepper relish

2 large red bell peppers

½ fennel bulb, trimmed

⅓ cup pitted black olives (preferably kalamatas)

1 tablespoon fresh lemon juice

1 tablespoon extra virgin olive oil

1 large garlic clove, minced

½ teaspoon freshly ground black pepper

Preparation time: 20 minutes
Marinating time: 30 minutes
Cooking time: 15 minutes

1 If using the rosemary stalks, pull off and reserve the leaves from the bottom end of each stalk, keeping a cluster of about 2½ inches of leaves at the top. Soak the rosemary stalks (or the wooden skewers if using instead) in water while you marinate the turkey.

2 Cut the turkey into 24 cubes, about 1½ inches each. Sprinkle the turkey with the salt and pepper and spread in a single layer in a shallow baking dish. In a small bowl, whisk the wine, lemon juice, garlic, rosemary, sage, thyme, and fennel seeds; whisk in the oil. Drizzle the marinade over the turkey and toss until all of the pieces are coated. Cover with plastic wrap and marinate in the refrigerate for 30 minutes, turning once.

3 Meanwhile, make the relish. Seed the red peppers and cut into ¼-inch dice. Trim the fennel bulb and cut into ¼-inch dice. Cut the olives into ¼-inch dice. In a medium-size bowl, mix the diced peppers, fennel, and olives with the lemon juice, oil, garlic, and pepper.

4 Preheat the grill or broiler to high. Alternately thread the marinated turkey pieces and the onions onto the soaked rosemary stalks or skewers. In a small saucepan, bring the remaining marinade to a boil over high heat.

5 Grill or broil the kebabs for about 12 minutes, basting often with the marinade, or until the turkey is cooked throughout and is golden brown. Serve 2 kebabs to each person, with about ½ cup of relish and a generous scoop of cooked couscous or wild rice.

Healthy tips

• Red peppers and fennel are both excellent sources of vitamin C, as well as beta-carotene, which the body converts into vitamin A. Both of these nutrients are powerful antioxidants that can help to counteract the damaging effects of free radicals and protect against many diseases, including cancer and heart disease.

• Fennel is low in calories. A ½-cup serving provides only 14 calories.

Each serving (2 skewers each) provides
calories 321, **total fat** 14g, saturated fat 2g, cholesterol 95mg, sodium 431mg, **total carbohydrate** 12g, dietary fiber 2g, protein 36g

✓✓✓	C
✓✓	niacin, B$_6$
✓	A, B$_2$, calcium, iron, magnesium, potassium, zinc, copper

More ideas

• Turkey-vegetable kebabs: Increase the rosemary stalks or wooden skewers to 12 (step 1). Increase the turkey to 1½ pounds and cut into 36 cubes (step 2). Alternately thread additional vegetables with the turkey and onions on the kebabs: 2 cups of zucchini slices (1 inch thick); 2 cups of fresh or frozen and thawed corn-on-the-cob pieces (1 inch thick); 2 cups of cherry tomatoes (step 4). Cook as directed in step 5 for 12 to 14 minutes or until the turkey is cooked throughout and the corn and zucchini are tender. This recipe makes 6 servings; 2 kebabs per person.

• Tomato and roasted pepper relish: Use roasted red peppers instead of fresh, and 1 cup of chopped tomatoes instead of fennel (step 3). To roast the peppers, cut into quarters, then grill or broil for 6 minutes or until the skins are charred. Let cool in a closed paper bag, then peel off the skin. Finely dice and stir into relish.

Sweet-and-sour chicken pancakes

Sweet-and-sour stir-fries are traditional in Chinese cooking. Wine, ketchup, and vinegar add the savory and sour flavors; while pineapple, bell peppers, and sugar, the sweet. All is folded up for serving into lacy pancakes.

Makes 4 servings (8 pancakes)

Pancake batter

1 cup all-purpose flour

¼ teaspoon *each* salt and black pepper

1 cup low-fat milk (2% milkfat)

¼ cup water

2 large eggs, beaten

Sweet and sour chicken

1 pound boneless skinless chicken breasts

3 tablespoons cornstarch

¼ cup low-sodium soy sauce

2 tablespoons peanut oil

2 large onions, slivered (2 cups)

2 large green bell peppers, cut into thin strips

½ cup dry white wine

2 tablespoons tomato ketchup

2 tablespoons white wine vinegar

2 tablespoons sugar

2 cups thin fresh pineapple wedges

½ cup sliced green onions

Preparation time: 30 minutes

Cooking time: 25 minutes

Each serving provides

calories 534, total fat 14g, saturated fat 4g, cholesterol 180mg, sodium 880mg, total carbohydrate 61g, dietary fiber 4g, protein 37g

✓✓✓	niacin,C
✓✓	B$_1$, B$_2$, B$_6$
✓	A, B$_{12}$, folate, calcium, iron, magnesium, potassium, zinc, copper, fiber

1 First, make the pancakes. Preheat the oven to the lowest setting; set out a baking sheet. In a medium-size bowl, mix the flour, salt, and pepper. Make a well in the center with your hands. In a large measuring cup, whisk the milk, water, and eggs until frothy. Pour into the well, all at once, and whisk until batter forms. Cover with plastic wrap and let stand while you make the filling.

2 Spray an 8-inch nonstick crêpe pan or skillet (with sloping sides) with cooking spray and heat over medium-high heat for 1 minute. Pour in about 3 tablespoons of batter, quickly tilting the pan so the batter spreads evenly over the bottom.

3 Cook the pancake over medium-high heat for 2 minutes, then loosen the edges with a spatula and flip it over. Cook the second side for about 30 seconds or just until set. Slide the pancake onto a baking sheet and top with wax paper. Repeat with the rest of the batter (you will have a stack of 8 pancakes separated with paper). Cover with foil; place in oven to keep warm.

4 Now, make the chicken filling. Cut the chicken into long thin strips, about 3 inches long and ½ inch wide, and place in a medium-size bowl. Add 2 tablespoons *each* of the cornstarch and soy sauce and toss until well coated.

5 In a wok or large skillet, heat 1 tablespoon of the oil over high heat. Add the onions and bell peppers; stir-fry for 3 minutes. Using a slotted spoon, transfer the vegetables to a plate.

6 Add the remaining tablespoon of oil to the wok, then stir in the chicken mixture. Stir-fry for 4 minutes or until cooked through. Transfer to the plate with the vegetables.

7 Stir the remaining 1 tablespoon of cornstarch into the wine and add to the skillet with the ketchup, vinegar, sugar, and the remaining 2 tablespoons of soy sauce. Whisk until the sauce boils and thickens. Return the vegetables and chicken to the skillet with the pineapple. Heat through until bubbly. Fill the pancakes with the chicken mixture, fold into quarters, and decorate with the green onions.

Healthy tips

• Eggs provide valuable amounts of protein and iron. The vitamin C in the pineapple helps the body absorb the iron, which is important in preventing anemia.

• Pineapple is high in soluble dietary fiber, which may help to control high blood cholesterol.

More ideas

- Chili chicken pancakes: When making the pancake batter, add 1 teaspoon of mild chili powder to the flour mixture (step 1). For the vegetables, use 1 large red bell pepper and only 1 large green bell pepper instead of 2 (step 5); cut into thin strips, then add to the wok or skillet with the onions. To make the chicken filling hotter, add 1 minced small fresh red chili pepper (without seeds and membrane) to the onions and the bell peppers in the skillet (step 5). When making the sauce, substitute ½ cup of dry red wine for the white wine (step 7). Substitute 2 tablespoons of bottled chili sauce for the ketchup. Use 2 tablespoons of red wine vinegar instead of the white vinegar.

- Chinese chicken pancakes: When making the pancake batter, add ½ teaspoon Chinese five-spice powder to the flour mixture (step 1). Substitute ½ cup of hoisin sauce for the soy sauce (steps 4 and 7).

Herbed chicken and apple burgers

Lighten up your burgers and add new flavor at the same time. First, use ground chicken instead of beef. Then, to boost the fiber and flavor even more, add grated apples, as well as fresh sage and thyme. Grill them, broil them, or even pan-fry them. Any way you choose to cook these burgers, you'll be glad you did!

Makes 4 servings

1 pound ground chicken

1 large red onion, finely chopped (1 cup)

⅓ cup plain dry bread crumbs

2 large green apples, such as Granny Smith (for a tart taste) or Golden Delicious (for a sweet taste), peeled and coarsely grated

1 tablespoon chopped fresh sage leaves

1 tablespoon fresh thyme leaves

¼ teaspoon salt

½ teaspoon freshly ground black pepper

To serve

¼ cup wholegrain Dijon mustard

1 tablespoon clear golden honey

4 hamburger buns, split

3 ounces watercress sprigs, large stalks discarded (about 1½ cups)

Preparation time: 20 minutes

Chilling time: 1 hour

Grilling or broiling time: 20 minutes

Each burger on a bun provides

calories 431, total fat 17g, saturated fat 4g, cholesterol 146mg, sodium 897mg, total carbohydrate 49g, dietary fiber 2g, protein 24g

✓✓	niacin, B₆
✓	B₁, B₂, C, calcium, iron, magnesium, potassium, zinc

1 In a large bowl, place the chicken, onion, bread crumbs, apples, sage, thyme, salt, and pepper. Using your hands, mix the ingredients together until the ingredients are distributed evenly throughout. Wet your hands, then divide the mixture into 4 equal portions and shape each into a burger about 4 inches in diameter and 1½ inches thick. Chill the burgers for 1 hour to firm up the meat and make it easier to hold together while it cooks.

2 Preheat the grill or broiler to high. Place burgers on a rack about 6 inches from the source of heat. Grill or broil the burgers, turning them one time, until they are golden brown on both sides and just until they are still juicy but cooked through completely.

3 While the burgers cook, mix the mustard and honey in a small cup. On a flat surface, open the 4 buns with the soft cut sides up. Spread the cut sides of both the tops and bottoms of the buns with the honey mustard. Pile one-fourth of the watercress on the bottom of each bun.

4 When the burgers are ready, transfer a burger to the bottom of each bun, placing it on top of the watercress. Cover with the top of the bun and serve immediately.

Healthy tips

● Apples provide good amounts of vitamin C and pectin, a soluble fiber. When you eat apples with their skins still on, you get even more fiber — one-third more, to be exact.

● Ounce for ounce, ground chicken has 48% less fat than lean ground beef.

More ideas

● Barbecued chicken burgers: Add ¼ cup of bottled barbecue sauce (choose the hotness you like) to the chicken mixture (beginning of step 1). If the mixture is too moist to shape, add an extra tablespoon of bread crumbs. Omit the honey mustard (step 3), and spread the rolls with a little extra barbecue sauce instead.

● Pan-fried burgers: Instead of grilling or broiling the burgers (step 2), heat 2 tablespoons of sunflower oil in a large skillet over medium-high heat. Add the burgers and cook about 3 to 4 minutes on each side or until brown, turning each burger one time. Reduce the heat to medium and cook the burgers about 12 to 14 minutes more or until they are cooked through completely.

main course poultry

Chicken fajitas with tomato salsa

The original Mexican fajitas are made by marinating skirt beefsteak for 24 hours, then grilling them, wrapping them in warm tortillas with peppers and onions, and serving with spicy salsa. Here, sizzling chicken strips replace the beef for a lower-fat variation of this Southwestern favorite. A fresh tomato salsa tops it all off.

Makes 6 servings

Chicken fajitas

1½ pounds boneless skinless chicken breasts

3 large limes (½ cup)

¼ cup chopped fresh coriander leaves

3 large garlic cloves, minced

2 to 3 teaspoons mild chili powder, to taste

1 teaspoon ground cumin

1 teaspoon paprika

3 tablespoons sunflower oil

3 large green or red bell peppers

2 extra-large yellow onions

12 flour tortillas (8 inches in diameter)

½ cup reduced-fat sour cream

Fresh coriander sprigs

Tomato salsa

1 cup chopped ripe tomatoes, diced

½ cup thinly sliced green onions

1 medium-hot fresh green chili pepper, seeded and minced

2 tablespoons fresh lemon juice

2 tablespoons tomato paste

1 tablespoon chopped fresh coriander leaves

2 large garlic cloves, minced

½ teaspoon ground cumin

Hot pepper sauce (optional)

Preparation time: 45 minutes

Marinating time: 30 minutes

Cooking time: 20 minutes

1 First, marinate the chicken, In a large shallow dish, arrange the chicken breasts in a single layer. In a small bowl, whisk 1 teaspoon of lime zest, the juice of the 3 limes (½ cup), the ¼ cup chopped coriander, the garlic, chili powder, cumin, paprika, and 2 tablespoons of the oil. Pour this mixture over the chicken, cover with plastic wrap, and let marinate in the refrigerator for at least 30 minutes.

2 Now, make the salsa. In a medium-size bowl, toss the tomatoes, green onions, minced chili pepper, lemon juice, tomato paste, the chopped coriander, garlic, and cumin. Taste the salsa and add a little hot pepper sauce if it's not hot enough.

3 Preheat the grill to high and preheat the oven to 350°F. Seed the bell peppers and peel the onions. Slice the peppers and the onions lengthwise into thin strips. Heat a large skillet (preferably a cast-iron one) over high heat until it is very hot. Brush with the remaining 1 tablespoon of oil. Add the bell peppers and onions and sauté for 8 minutes or until the onions are brown. Remove the skillet from the heat, leave vegetables in the pan, and keep hot.

4 Divide the tortillas into 2 stacks, wrap each stack in foil, and keep warm in the oven for 10 minutes.

Meanwhile, grill the chicken 6 inches from the heat for about 10 minutes, turning once, or until the juices of the chicken run clear when a breast is pierced with a fork. Cut the chicken into long strips, 1 inch wide.

5 To serve, divide the chicken, onions, and peppers among the warm tortillas and roll up. Garnish with sprigs of coriander and serve with the fresh salsa and sour cream.

Healthy tips

- Garlic has been used throughout history as a cure-all. Recent research has found that it can help lower blood lipids, thus reducing the risk of heart disease. Garlic can also act an an antioxidant and lengthens blood clotting times.
- The vitamin C in the tomatoes helps the body absorb the iron from the chicken.

Each serving of 2 fajitas provides
calories 522, total fat 17g, saturated fat 2g, cholesterol 75mg, sodium 468mg, total carbohydrate 59g, dietary fiber 4g, protein 35g

✓✓✓	niacin, C
✓✓	B$_1$, B$_6$
✓	A, B$_2$, folate, calcium, iron, magnesium, potassium, zinc, copper, fiber

Another idea

• Chicken-Cheddar Quesadillas: Prepare chicken, peppers, and onions as directed through step 4. Use only 9 tortillas. Preheat the oven to 350°F but do not warm the tortillas. Instead, on an ungreased baking sheet, make 3 stacked quesadillas. For each stack: top a tortilla with one-sixth *each* of the grilled chicken and the sautéed bell peppers and onions; sprinkle with 2 heaping tablespoons of shredded sharp Cheddar cheese. Cover with a second tortilla and repeat with one-sixth more of the chicken, bell peppers, and onions and 2 more heaping tablespoons of Cheddar. Top with a third tortilla, pressing down lightly. Bake the quesadilla stacks for 5 minutes or until the cheese melts and the tortillas are slightly crisp. Cut each stack in half and serve with the salsa and sour cream.

121

Super Sandwiches

Pitas, calzones, tostadas, rolls, and bagels

FOR TASTY TERRIFIC SANDWICHES, poultry tops the list. Spread soft rolls with honey mustard and stuff with roasted chicken thighs. Roll up strips of chicken, broccoli florets, and cashews in the pancake-like breads of India called chapatis. Spoon shreds of chili-spiced chicken and pinto beans onto crisp tacos. Stuff pitas, as they do in Greece, with spicy chicken strips, fresh greens, and *tzatziki,* a cucumber-yogurt sauce. Serve slices of roasted turkey on bagels under melted Stilton. Bake chicken with roasted peppers and cheese in turnovers made from pizza dough. Or pack a picnic with a hollowed-out country loaf stuffed with turkey, pesto, and peppery greens.

Greek chicken pitas

For a chicken sandwich with a delicious difference, stuff Middle Eastern pocket breads (pitas) with spicy sautéed chicken strips, some tender gourmet lettuce leaves (mesclun), and a generous helping of the Greek cucumber and yogurt sauce called tzatziki. *Another day, spice the chicken with chili seasonings and cook on the grill.*

Makes 4 stuffed pita sandwiches

Chicken pitas

1¼ pounds boneless skinless chicken breasts

½ cup instant polenta (uncooked)

1 tablespoon freeze-dried onion flakes

1 teaspoon paprika

¾ teaspoon cumin seeds

½ teaspoon coarsely ground black pepper

¼ teaspoon salt

2 tablespoons extra virgin olive oil

4 pita breads with pockets (6 inches)

2 cups mesclun salad greens

Tzatziki (cucumber-yogurt sauce)

½ medium cucumber

½ cup plain low-fat yogurt

½ cup plain whole-milk yogurt

1 large garlic clove, minced

1 tablespoon chopped fresh mint

1 teaspoon bottled mint sauce or mint jelly

Preparation time: 25 minutes

Cooking time: about 8 minutes

Each pita sandwich provides

calories 514, **total fat** 13g, **saturated fat** 3g, **cholesterol** 92mg, **sodium** 568mg, **total carbohydrate** 55g, **dietary fiber** 2g, **protein** 42g

✓✓✓	niacin
✓✓	B₁, B₂, B₆
✓	A, B₁₂, folate, C, calcium, iron, magnesium, potassium, zinc, copper

1 First, prepare the chicken. Cut the chicken into strips, about 3 or 4 inches long and 1 inch wide. In a self-sealing plastic bag, place the polenta, onion flakes, paprika, cumin seeds, pepper, and salt; close the bag and shake until well mixed. Add the chicken strips, a few at a time, and toss well to coat all over. Shake off any excess coating and transfer the chicken strips to a plate.

2 Now, make the *tzatziki* sauce. Grate the cucumber (do not peel) and squeeze out any excess moisture with your hands. Place in a small bowl with all of the remaining sauce ingredients. Stir until well blended. Refrigerate while you cook the chicken.

3 While the sauce chills, prepare the pitas. Preheat the oven to 350°F. In a large skillet, heat 1 tablespoon of the oil over medium-high heat, swirling the oil around the pan until it is lightly coated. Add half the coated chicken strips and stir-fry for 3 minutes or until golden brown and cooked through. Transfer the strips to a plate lined with paper towels and keep hot. Repeat, using the rest of the oil and cooking the rest of the chicken.

4 Meanwhile, place the pita breads directly on the oven rack to warm for 1 or 2 minutes on each side.

5 To assemble each of the 4 sandwiches, fill a pita pocket with one-fourth of the salad greens. Pile in one-fourth of the chicken strips and spoon over about ¼ cup of the *tzatziki* sauce. Serve immediately, as the pitas can get soggy upon standing.

Healthy tips

● Yogurt is an excellent source of both calcium and phosphorus. The amount of fat in a spoonful of yogurt reflects the amount of fat that the milk it is made from (either whole or low-fat). Naturally, plain whole-milk yogurt is higher in fat than plain low-fat yogurt: ½ cup of plain whole-milk yogurt has 4 grams of fat, in comparison to only 2 grams of fat in ½ cup of plain low-fat yogurt. By combining the two types of yogurts, as in this recipe, you reduce the fat 25%, tablespoon by tablespoon.

● Adopt the habit of stuffing fresh greens into sandwiches. They are low in fat and high in fiber.

super sandwiches

More ideas

- Grilled chicken pitas: Buy 4 boneless skinless chicken breast halves (about 5 ounces each); do not cut them into strips (step 1). When preparing the seasoning mixture in the plastic bag, omit the polenta (step 1). Instead of preheating the oven (step 3), preheat the grill or broiler to high. Omit the oil. Cook the chicken breasts, 6 inches from the heat, for 15 minutes, turning once, or until the juices of the chicken run clear when a breast is pierced with a fork. During the last 2 minutes of grilling, warm the pitas on the grill rack instead of the oven rack (step 4), turning once. Assemble each of the 4 pitas as in step 5, substituting 1 grilled chicken breast half for the chicken strips.

- Chili-chicken pitas with hot tomato salsa: Follow directions for grilled chicken pitas (at left), adding 2 teaspoons chili powder to the seasoning mixture. Substitute the Tomato Salsa (see page 120) for the *tzatziki*.

- If you cannot find freeze-dried onions, use onion salt and omit the ½ teaspoon salt.

- For extra fiber, buy whole-wheat pitas.

Hot turkey and Stilton bagels

Slices of fresh roasted turkey make delicious sandwiches. To make it easier to slice the meat very thin, place the roasted meat in the freezer for about half an hour. Stack the turkey on fresh toasted bagels spread with cranberry jelly and crumble Stilton cheese on top. Pop under the broiler until the cheese melts and serve open-faced.

Makes 4 open-faced bagel sandwiches

4 bagels, plain or onion flavored

3 tablespoons unsalted butter, melted

1 cup canned cranberry jelly

12 ounces cold roasted turkey breasts
   (boneless and skinless), sliced very thin

4 ounces Stilton or blue cheese

To serve

2 large oranges, cut into wedges

2 cups curly leaf lettuce

Preparation time: 20 minutes

Cooking time: 5 minutes

1 First, toast the bagels. Preheat the broiler. Using a serrated bread knife, cut the bagels in half horizontally and brush the cut sides with the melted butter. Place the bagels on a baking sheet and lightly toast both sides for about 1 minute per side.

2 Now, assemble the 4 sandwiches. For each one, spread cranberry jelly on the cut sides of both bagel halves. Pile turkey slices on both halves and crumble the Stilton cheese on top (use one-fourth of the turkey and one-fourth of the cheese for each sandwich).

3 Return to the broiler to cook for 1 to 2 minutes, just to melt the cheese (watch closely!). Serve hot, with the orange wedges and salad leaves.

More ideas

● Smoked turkey and Camembert on cinnamon-raisin bagels: Use 4 cinnamon-raisin bagels instead of plain or onion-flavored ones (step 1). Substitute 4 ounces of Camembert cheese for the Stilton (step 2). Be sure to chill the cheese well before slicing it. Substitute 12 ounces of cooked smoked turkey breasts for the plain turkey breasts (step 2).

● Hot turkey and Gruyère on sesame bagels: Use 4 sesame-seed bagels instead of plain or onion-flavored ones (step 1). Use 1 cup of red pepper relish instead of the cranberry jelly (step 2). Substitute 4 ounces of Gruyère cheese for the Stilton (step 2).

● Hot turkey and Gorgonzola on onion bagels: Use 4 onion-flavored bagels, instead of plain ones (step 1). Substitute 1 cup of unpeeled thin red apple slices for the cranberry jelly (step 2). Substitute 4 ounces of Gorgonzola cheese for the Stilton (step 2).

● Bagels are doughnut-shaped yeast rolls that are first boiled before they are baked. Traditionally, in Jewish and Eastern European communities, bagels are made from a high-gluten white flour. Today however, many flavors are readily found in supermarkets, bakeries, and specialty bagel shops. For this sandwich, try different ones: pumpernickel, sun-dried tomato, caraway, whole-wheat.

Healthy tips

● Although Stilton is relatively high in fat, it has a strong flavor, so a little goes a long way. Like all cheese, it is a good source of protein and a valuable source of calcium, and the B vitamins of riboflavin and B_{12}.

● Bread is a very important part of a healthy diet, as it provides complex carbohydrates, and many B vitamins and iron.

Each bagel sandwich provides

calories 625, total fat 19g, saturated fat 11g, cholesterol 115mg, sodium 842mg, total carbohydrate 75g, dietary fiber 3g, protein 40g

✓✓✓	niacin, C
✓✓	B_1, B_2, B_6, calcium, iron
✓	A, B_{12}, folate, magnesium, potassium, zinc, copper, fiber

super sandwiches

Sweet roasted chicken rolls

Throughout England and Scotland, soft white yeast rolls (called "baps"), typically with a little flour dusted on top, are eaten hot at breakfast. For these sandwiches, soft potato rolls or English muffins make great substitutes. Stuff them with roasted chicken thighs, seasoned with honey mustard and topped with mangoes and romaine.

Makes 4 sandwiches

4 boneless skinless chicken thighs
   (4 ounces each)
6 tablespoons whole-grain mustard
2 tablespoons golden honey
½ teaspoon freshly ground black pepper
¼ teaspoon salt
4 large soft rolls or English muffins
8 romaine lettuce leaves
1 large ripe mango or 2 large ripe peaches,
   peeled, pitted, and sliced ¼ inch thick
4 green onions, thinly sliced (½ cup)

Preparation time: 20 minutes
Roasting time: 20 minutes

Each sandwich provides

calories 348, total fat 7g, saturated fat 2g, cholesterol 46mg, sodium 999mg, total carbohydrate 53g, dietary fiber 2g, protein 18g

✓✓	A, niacin, C
✓	B$_1$, B$_2$, B$_6$, folate, calcium, iron, potassium, zinc, copper

1 Preheat the oven to 350°F and oil a large shallow ovenproof baking dish, large enough to hold the chicken thighs once they've been flattened out. Mix the mustard and honey together.

2 Now, roast the chicken. Using a boning knife, make a lengthwise slit halfway through each thigh and open up like a book. Press down to flatten them out, then sprinkle both sides with the pepper and salt. Place the thighs, smooth-side up, in the baking dish. Reserve half of the honey mustard for the sandwiches; spread the rest over the top of the chicken thighs. Roast the thighs, uncovered, for 20 minutes or until the juices of the chicken run clear when a thigh is pierced with a fork.

3 Meanwhile, split open the rolls or muffins and toast them on the oven rack for about 4 minutes or until lightly golden. Remove from the oven and spread the cut sides of the warm rolls with the reserved honey mustard.

4 For each sandwich, place 1 lettuce leaf on the bottom half of each roll. Layer one-fourth of the mango slices, one-fourth of the green onions, 1 roasted chicken thigh, and 1 more lettuce leaf. Cover with the top of the roll, pressing down slightly to close. Serve the sandwiches immediately.

More ideas

● Cajun chicken po'boys: Omit the honey mustard (step 1). Replace with hot pepper mayo made by mixing ½ cup of reduced-fat mayonnaise with 1 tablespoon of hot pepper sauce. Substitute 4 French baguettes for the soft rolls (step 3). After toasting, line each baguette with 1 one-ounce slice of jalapeño reduced-fat cheese (4 ounces total). Shred the lettuce; omit the mangoes; substitute ½ cup of slivered yellow onion and ½ cup of thin green pepper strips for the mangoes (step 4).

● Mangia! heroes: For the seasoned mustard, substitute 2 large cloves of minced garlic for the honey (step 1). Substitute 4 Italian rolls for the soft rolls (step 3). Replace the mango slices with 1 cup of pickled antipasto vegetables (found in the pickle aisle of the supermarket). Substitute ½ cup of red onion slivers for the green onions (step 4).

● Replace the mangoes with 1 cup of roasted red pepper strips (roast with the chicken).

Healthy tip

● Compared to mayonnaise, whole-grain mustard has 85% fewer calories, plus it does not contain any oil or fat. One tablespoon of whole-grain mustard has only 15 calories and 0 grams of fat, while 1 tablespoon of mayonnaise contains 100 calories and 11 grams of fat.

Chicken and broccoli chapatis

These mouthwatering, pancake-like breads are one of the simplest and most healthful breads found in India.

Chapatis are made from whole-wheat flour and water (no yeast), then baked on a dry griddle without any fat.

Fill them with this chicken, broccoli, and cashew mixture, and supper is served — traditionally, as in India.

Makes 4 rolled sandwiches

Yogurt-vegetable salad

1 recipe raita (see page 72)

Chicken Chapatis

12 ounces cooked chicken breasts
  (boneless and skinless, 2 cups)

1 tablespoon sunflower oil

3 cups fresh broccoli florets, coarsely
  chopped

½ cup unsalted cashews, coarsely chopped

2 teaspoons grated fresh gingerroot

1 large garlic clove, minced

¼ cup bottled mango chutney

½ teaspoon freshly ground black pepper

4 chapatis (about 10 inches in diameter)
  or 4 pitas (about 8 inches in diameter)

Preparation time: 30 minutes
Cooking time: 18 minutes

Each chapati provides

calories 523, total fat 21g, saturated fat 4g,
cholesterol 77mg, sodium 283mg, total
carbohydrate 46g, dietary fiber 5g, protein 39g

✓✓✓	niacin, C
✓✓	B₂, B₆, magnesium, potassium, copper
✓	A, B₁, B₁₂, folate, calcium, iron, zinc, fiber

1 First, prepare the raita, according to the recipe, and refrigerate.

2 Now, prepare the chapati filling. Cut the chicken into bite-size pieces. In a large skillet, heat the oil over medium-high heat. Add the broccoli, cashews, gingerroot, and garlic and stir-fry for 4 minutes or just until the broccoli is crisp-tender.

3 Add the chicken, chutney, and pepper to the broccoli mixture. Stir-fry 3 minutes more or until the chicken is cooked and turns opaque.

4 Meanwhile, coat a nonstick griddle or a medium-size nonstick skillet with cooking spray and heat until hot. Sprinkle the chapatis with a little water and heat for 2 minutes on each side or until hot. Keep hot.

5 For each chapati, spoon one-fourth of the chicken-broccoli mixture across one end of the chapati, stopping within ½ inch of the edge, then roll it up. (Or stuff into pitas.) Serve the chapatis hot with the raita on the side.

Another idea

● Chicken-chili enchiladas: Replace the chicken-broccoli filling with Mexican chicken: Preheat the oven to 350°F. In a large nonstick skillet, heat 2 tablespoons of vegetable oil. Add 1½ pounds of uncooked skinless chicken breast strips (4 inches long and 1 inch wide), 1 cup of yellow onion strips, and 1 teaspoon *each* of chili powder, cumin seeds, and coriander. Sauté for 5 minutes or until the chicken turns opaque. Stir in 2 cups *each* of green bell pepper strips and red bell pepper strips and continue sautéing 8 minutes more or until the peppers are tender; remove from the heat. Meanwhile, heat 8 ten-inch flour tortillas instead of chapatis, according to the directions in step 4. For each enchilada, use one-eighth of the chicken-chili mixture and roll up as in step 5. Place all 8 enchiladas seam-side down in a bake dish, sprinkle with ½ cup of shredded Cheddar cheese, and bake for 15 minutes until piping hot. Serve with chunky tomato salsa. Makes 4 servings.

Healthy tips

● Broccoli is packed with vitamins. It is an excellent source of the antioxidants beta-carotene and vitamin C. Just 1 cup of cooked broccoli provides over 100% of the Daily Value (DV) for vitamin C and 20% of the DV for vitamin A, folate, and fiber.
● Like other members of the Cruciferae cabbage family of vegetables (such as cauliflower, Brussels sprouts, cabbage, and kale), broccoli contains a number of different phytochemicals. One of these, indoles, may help to protect against breast cancer by inhibiting the action of the estrogens that trigger the growth of tumors.

super sandwiches

Mexican tostadas

Tostada comes from the Spanish word meaning "toasted". In Mexico it refers to flat, crisply fried corn tortillas, topped with all sorts of savory things — usually beans, shreds of chicken, lettuce, and cheese, plus diced tomatoes and sour cream. Here, spicy tomato sauce and pinto beans replace the traditional refried beans.

Makes 8 tostadas

2 whole chicken breasts on the bone
  (2 pounds)
2 tablespoons safflower oil
2 large red or green bell peppers, seeded and
  coarsely chopped (3 cups)
2 large yellow onions, coarsely chopped
  (2 cups)
2 large garlic cloves, thinly sliced
1 tablespoon chili powder (mild to medium)
2 teaspoons paprika
1 teaspoon ground cumin
½ teaspoon freshly ground black pepper
¼ teaspoon salt
1 can chopped tomatoes with juice, no salt
  added (15 ounces)
¼ teaspoon sugar
1 can pinto beans (15 ounces), undrained
8 soft corn tortillas (about 6 inches)

To serve

2 large tomatoes, cut into 1-inch dice
  (2 cups)
2 cups shredded iceberg lettuce
4 pickled jalapeño chilies, coarsely chopped
½ cup shredded Cheddar cheese (optional)
½ cup sour cream (optional)
2 radishes, sliced (optional)
Bottled chunky tomato salsa (optional)

Preparation time: 30 minutes
Cooking time: 50 minutes

1 First, cook the chicken. In a large saucepan, place the chicken breasts; add enough cold water to cover. Bring to a boil over high heat, then reduce the heat to medium-low and simmer, uncovered, for 20 minutes. Using a slotted spoon, transfer the chicken to a rack to cool. When cool enough to handle, remove the meat from the bones, discarding both the skin and bones. Shred the meat and set aside.

2 Now, cook the vegetables. In a large skillet, heat 1 tablespoon of the oil over medium-high heat. Add the peppers, onions, and garlic. Sauté for 8 minutes or until softened. Stir in the chili powder, paprika, cumin, pepper, and salt; cook 2 minutes more. Stir in the tomatoes with their juice and the sugar. Simmer, uncovered, 8 minutes more or until the sauce thickens. Remove from the heat and keep warm. Meanwhile, in a small saucepan, heat the beans over medium heat in their liquid; drain well.

3 In a heavy skillet (use an cast-iron skillet if you have one), heat the remaining oil and toast the tortillas, one at a time, over high heat, about 1 minute on each side or until slightly crisp and lightly browned. Keep hot in foil.

4 To assemble each of the 8 tostadas, spoon on top of a tortilla about ¼ cup *each* of the tomato sauce, beans, chicken, diced tomato, and lettuce. Sprinkle with a few jalapeños. Top with 1 tablespoon *each* of the Cheddar cheese and sour cream, plus a radish slice, and some salsa, if you wish.

Another idea

● Substitute 2 cups of fresh or frozen corn kernels (cooked and drained) for the beans (end of step 2).

Healthy tip

● Dried beans, peas, and lentils are an excellent source of protein and a good source of soluble dietary fiber. They are even a better source when they are eaten with grains, such as the wheat or maize found in these corn tortillas.

Each tostada provides

calories 268, total fat 7g, saturated fat 1g, cholesterol 44mg, sodium 519mg, total carbohydrate 31g, dietary fiber 4g, protein 22g

✓✓✓	C
✓✓	niacin, B$_6$,
✓	A, B$_1$, folate, calcium, iron, magnesium, potassium, copper, fiber

Calzones with roasted peppers

Imagine an individual stuffed pizza folded over into a semicircle and baked as a turnover — and you have a traditional calzone. Here, ready-to-use refrigerated pizza crust is substituted for homemade yeast dough, which requires mixing and rising time. Stuff with diced chicken, olives, roasted peppers, fresh basil, and mozzarella.

Makes 6 calzones

- 3 large red bell peppers, halved and seeded
- 1 tablespoon extra virgin olive oil
- 2 large red onions, slivered (2 cups)
- 3 large garlic cloves, minced
- 1½ pounds boneless skinless chicken breasts, cut into bite-size pieces
- ½ teaspoon freshly ground black pepper
- 12 sun-dried tomato halves packed in oil, drained and chopped
- ½ cup slivered fresh basil leaves
- ½ cup sliced pitted black olives
- 8 ounces shredded part-skim mozzarella cheese (1 cup)
- 2 packages refrigerated pizza crust dough (10 ounces each)
- 1 large egg, lightly beaten
- 2 tablespoons sesame seeds

Preparation time: 45 minutes
Baking time: 15 minutes

Each calzone provides

calories 449, total fat 21g, saturated fat 6g, cholesterol 126mg, sodium 908mg, total carbohydrate 57g, dietary fiber 3g, protein 47g

✓✓✓	niacin, C
✓✓	B₆, calcium
✓	A, B₁, B₂, B₁₂, iron, magnesium, potassium, zinc, copper, fiber

1 First, roast the peppers. Preheat the oven to 425°F and lightly oil a baking sheet (preferably a nonstick one). Place the peppers on the tray, cut-side down, and roast for 15 minutes or until the skins are very dark. Transfer peppers to a paper bag and close tightly; set aside to cool. Leave the oven on; clean off and oil the baking sheet again.

2 Meanwhile, prepare the filling. In a large skillet, heat the oil over medium-high heat. Add the onions and garlic and sauté for 5 minutes or until soft and golden.

3 Toss the chicken with the pepper, add to the skillet mixture, and stir-fry 2 minutes more or just until the meat turns opaque. Remove from the heat and stir in the tomatoes, basil, and olives. Peel off and discard the dark skins from the peppers and finely chop. Stir into the chicken mixture in the skillet, along with the mozzarella.

4 Now, shape and fill the calzones. On a lightly floured flat surface, place 1 of the rolls of pizza dough and cut it into 3 equal pieces. Using a rolling pin, roll out each piece into an 8-inch round, about ⅛ inch thick. Repeat with the second roll of dough, making a total of 6 circles of dough.

5 For each of the 6 calzones, spoon one-sixth of the chicken mixture on one-half of each dough round, mounding the filling near the center and up to 1 inch from the edge.

6 Brush the edges of each dough round with beaten egg, then fold over into a semicircle. Pinch and flute the edges, sealing tightly. Place the calzones on the oiled baking sheet and cover with a clean towel. Let the calzones rise in a warm place for 15 minutes or until doubled in size.

7 Uncover the calzones, brush the tops and sides with the beaten egg, and sprinkle with the sesame seeds. Bake for 15 minutes or until golden.

Another idea

● Spanish empanadas: Add 4 ounces (¾ cup) of thinly sliced chorizo sausage to the skillet with the chicken (step 3), stir-frying 4 minutes instead of 2. Substitute 3 tablespoons of bottled chili sauce for the sun-dried tomatoes, ¼ cup of fresh marjoram leaves for the basil, and ½ cup of sliced pimiento-stuffed green olives for the black olives (step 3). Omit the mozzarella.

Healthy tip

● Red peppers are an excellent source of vitamin C. Even when roasted, as in this recipe, useful amounts of the vitamin remain.

Avocado chicken club sandwiches

In late 19th-century America, the club sandwich was a favorite in the train club cars, as well as men's private clubhouses. The first club sandwiches were not triple-deckers, as is the custom today. Instead, they used only two pieces of toast with roasted chicken, lettuce, bacon, and tomatoes stuffed between them. Here, a tasty variation.

Makes 4 club sandwiches

12 slices multigrain bread

½ cup reduced-calorie mayonnaise

½ teaspoon coarsely ground black pepper

4 ounces prosciutto, cut into strips

1 large ripe avocado

2 tablespoons fresh lime juice

2 cups finely shredded iceberg lettuce

1 pound roasted chicken breasts (boneless and skinless), sliced thin

1 cup orange sections, coarsely chopped

1 bunch of watercress, tough stalks discarded (2 cups)

½ cup alfalfa sprouts

2 teaspoons sunflower seeds, toasted

Preparation time: 30 minutes
Cooking time: 3 minutes

Each triple-layer club sandwich provides

calories 636, total fat 27g, saturated fat 5g, cholesterol 115mg, sodium 833mg, total carbohydrate 50g, dietary fiber 4g, protein 52g

✓✓✓	B₁, niacin, B₆, C, E
✓✓	B₂, folate, iron, magnesium, potassium
✓	A, B₁₂, calcium, zinc, copper, fiber

1 On a flat surface, spread out all 12 slices of the bread. In a cup, mix the mayonnaise with the pepper; spread about 2 teaspoons of the mayonnaise on the top side of each slice of bread.

2 Heat a large empty skillet over high heat for 1 minute. Add the strips of prosciutto and sauté for 2 minutes or until crisp and curly. Remove from heat.

3 Peel the avocado and remove the seed. Using a fork, mash the avocado in a small bowl and mix with the lime juice.

4 For each club sandwich, start with 1 slice of bread, mayonnaise-side up. Layer on ½ cup of the shredded lettuce, one-fourth of the roasted chicken slices and one-fourth of the prosciutto strips. Cover with a second slice of bread, mayonnaise-side down.

5 Spread one-fourth of the avocado on top of this second slice of bread. Layer with one-fourth of the oranges, watercress, and sprouts. Sprinkle each sandwich with ½ teaspoon of the sunflower seeds. Cover with a third slice of bread, mayonnaise-side down. Press down gently, then diagonally cut each sandwich into quarters for serving.

Another idea

• The all-American club: Substitute 12 thick slices of country white bread for the multigrain bread; toast both sides (step 1). Substitute 12 slices turkey bacon for the prosciutto; increase cooking time to 5 minutes (step 2). Use 3 slices of bacon for each sandwich (step 4). Omit the orange sections, watercress, sprouts, and sunflower seeds (step 5). Instead, substitute with 4 one-ounce slices of American cheese and 2 large ripe beefsteak tomatoes, sliced crosswise, ½ inch thick. Place 1 slice of cheese on the top of the avocado spread on the second slice of bread. Cover with one-fourth of the tomato slices and the third slice of bread, mayonnaise-side down (step 5).

Healthy tips

• Avocados have a reputation for being a "fatty" fruit, but most of their fat is of the good monounsaturated type.

• Sunflower seeds contain a good amount of vitamin E, which is one of the body's best antioxidants. It helps protect vitamin A, cell membranes, and polyunsaturated fats from oxidation. Sunflower seeds are also a good source of thiamine.

super sandwiches

Provençal turkey sandwiches

In Provence, a hearty sandwich of cold meats, lettuces, and other salad vegetables packed inside a hollowed-out bread loaf was traditionally carried into the fields by the workers. This meal-in-a-loaf gave them plenty of the protein and carbohydrates they needed. This updated version features low-fat roasted turkey and fragrant pesto.

Makes 4 sandwiches

- 1 rustic crusty white round loaf of bread, about 8 inches in diameter (1 pound)
- ½ cup pesto sauce (purchased or homemade)
- 2 cups arugula, trimmed
- 1 cup watercress leaves, stems trimmed
- 2 large beefsteak tomatoes (1 pound total), sliced crosswise, ½ inch thick
- ½ teaspoon salt
- ½ teaspoon freshly ground black pepper
- 1 large avocado
- 2 tablespoons fresh lemon juice
- 1 pound roasted turkey breasts, (boneless and skinless), sliced thick

Preparation time: 30 minutes
Chilling time: 1 hour

Each sandwich (¼ of loaf) provides
calories 526, total fat 28g, saturated fat 5g, cholesterol 101mg, sodium 764mg, total carbohydrate 27g, dietary fiber 3g, protein 43g

✓✓✓	niacin, C
✓✓	B₆, potassium
✓	A, B₁, B₂, folate, calcium, iron, magnesium, zinc, copper, fiber

1 First, hollow out the bread. Using a bread knife and cutting crosswise, about 2 inches below the top, slice the top off the loaf of bread. Remove the soft bread from the underside of the lid and from the center of the loaf, leaving a shell about ¾ inch thick. Spread the pesto evenly over the underside of the lid and the inside of the loaf shell.

2 Now, fill the sandwich. In a self-sealing plastic bag, place the arugula and watercress; shake to mix well. Inside the bread shell, stack half of the tomato slices on the bottom of the shell; sprinkle with half of the salt and pepper. Cover the tomatoes with half of the arugula-watercress mixture.

3 Peel the avocado, cut it in half, lift out the seed, then slice lengthwise, ½ inch thick. Immediately, sprinkle the avocado slices with the lemon juice, then arrange in a layer over the greens. Layer the sliced turkey on top of the avocado and sprinkle with the rest of the salt and pepper. Arrange the remaining tomato slices, then the rest of the greens, on top. Press the sandwich filling down gently with your hands, then replace the top of the loaf.

4 Wrap the loaf in plastic wrap and refrigerate for at least 1 hour, but not more than 2 hours. Cut the loaf into 4 equal servings.

More ideas

- Substitute black olive paste (tapenade) or hot pepper relish for the pesto (step 1).
- Cover the sliced turkey with 2 cups of grilled eggplant slices and sprinkle with a little garlic-flavored olive oil before sprinkling with the rest of the salt and pepper (step 3).
- Make individual sandwiches with 4 large sourdough rolls or soft potato rolls.

Healthy tips
- The health benefits of eating watercress have been acknowledged for many centuries. Hippocrates wrote about its medicinal value in 460 B.C. and built the world's first hospital next to a stream so he could grow fresh watercress for his patients. Watercress provides good amounts of several antioxidants, including vitamin C and carotenoid compounds.
- Enriched bread has the B vitamins of thiamine, riboflavin, niacin, and folate, as well as iron, added to it.

A glossary of nutritional terms

Antioxidant These are compounds that help to protect the body's cells against the damaging effects of free radicals. Vitamins C and E, beta-carotene (the plant form of vitamin A), and the mineral selenium, together with many of the phytochemicals found in fruit and vegetables, all act as antioxidants.

Calorie A unit used to measure the energy value of food and the intake and use of energy by the body. The scientific definition of 1 calorie is the amount of heat required to raise the temperature of 1 gram of water by 1 degree centigrade. The term kilocalories (abbreviated to *kcal*) is equivalent to 1,000 calories. A person's energy (calorie) requirement varies based on his or her age, sex, and level of activity. *(See also Pyramid, pages 6 and 7.)*

Carbohydrates These substances provide about half of the energy needs for the body. Carbohydrates are divided into two groups: simple carbohydrates, or sugars; and the complex carbohydrates, or starches and fibers. The sugars come mainly from foods of plant origin except for lactose, which comes from milk and milk products.

Sugars are digested and absorbed rapidly to provide energy very quickly. Fructose, the sweetest of sugars, occurs naturally in fruits and honey.

Complex carbohydrates are long chains of the simple sugar called glucose. Plant cells store glucose as starches just as the body stores glucose as glycogen. All starchy foods come from plants. Starches are digested more slowly than sugars. The best food sources include grains and grain products, such as bread, cereals, corn, pasta, potatoes, rice, and other starchy vegetables (sweet potatoes and parsnips).

Fibers are the structural parts of plants that are not digested by the human digestive enzymes. *(See also Fiber, this page, right column.)*

Daily Values

Total Fat	65 grams
Saturated Fat	20 grams
Cholesterol	300 mg
Sodium	2,400 mg
Carbohydrate	300 grams
Dietary Fiber	25 grams
Protein	50 grams
Vitamin A	5,000 IU or 1,500 µg RE
Vitamin B$_1$ (thiamine)	1.5 mg
Vitamin B$_2$ (riboflavin)	1.7 mg
Niacin (Niacin Equivalent/NE)	20 mg
Vitamin B$_6$	2 mg
Vitamin B$_{12}$	6 µg
Folate	400 µg
Vitamin C	60 mg
Vitamin D	400 IU or 10 µg
Vitamin E	30 IU or 9 mg α-TE
Calcium	1,000 mg
Iron	18 mg
Magnesium	400 mg
Potassium	3,500 mg
Zinc	15 mg
Copper	2 mg

Cholesterol An integral part of cell membranes, cholesterol is a waxy substance that is important to many body compounds such as bile, acids, sex hormones, adrenal hormones, and vitamin D. Cholesterol made by the body is called blood cholesterol. Cholesterol, found only in foods of animal origin, is referred to as dietary cholesterol. High blood cholesterol levels are an important risk factor for coronary heart disease, but the liver makes most of the cholesterol in our blood—only 25% comes from cholesterol in food. So the best way to reduce blood cholesterol is to eat less saturated fat and to increase your intake of foods containing soluble fiber. Recommended intake level is 300 milligrams daily.

Daily Values (DV) Frequently appearing on food labels, Daily Values are standard values of nutrients for adults and children over 4 years old. Developed by the Food and Drug Administration (FDA), they are based on the Recommended Dietary Allowances (RDA). They also include information on other food components, such as fat and fiber.

Dietary Guidelines for Americans (1995) Healthy eating guidelines that were developed for healthy people over the age of two years by the U.S. Department of Agriculture (USDA) and the U.S. Department of Health and Human Services. *(For Guidelines, see page 6.)*

Fat Although a small amount of fat is essential for good health, many people consume far too much. Healthy eating guidelines recommend that no more than 30% of our daily energy intake (calories), or 65 grams per a 2,000 calorie diet, should come from fat. Each gram of fat contains 9 kcal, more than twice as many calories as carbohydrates or protein.

Fats can be divided into three main groups: saturated, monounsaturated, and polyunsaturated. *Saturated fatty acids* are found mainly in animal fats, such as butter and other dairy products and in fatty meat. A high intake of saturated fat is known to be a risk factor for coronary heart disease and certain types of cancer. Current guidelines are that no more than 10% of our daily calories should come from saturated fats, which is about 20 grams in a 2,000 calorie diet.

Where saturated fats tend to be solid at room temperature, the *unsaturated fatty acids*—monounsaturated and polyunsaturated—tend to be liquid. *Monounsaturated fats* are found predominantly in olive oil, peanut oil, rapeseed oil, and avocados. Foods high in *polyunsaturates* include most vegetable oils; the exceptions are saturated palm oil and coconut oil.

The body can make both saturated and monounsaturated fatty acids, but certain polyunsaturated fatty acids, known as *essential fatty acids*, must be supplied by food. There are two "families" of these fatty acids: *omega-6*, derived from linoleic acid, and *omega-3*, from linolenic acid. The main food sources of the *omega-6* family are vegetable oils (such as corn, safflower, soybean), and sunflower seeds, nuts, and leafy vegetables. *Omega-3* fatty acids are provided by oily fish, nuts, and vegetable oils, such as soybean and canola.

Fiber Technically non-starch polysaccharides (NSP), fiber is the term commonly used to describe several different compounds, such as pectin, hemicellulose, lignin, and gums, which are found in the cell walls of all plants. The body cannot digest fiber, but it plays an important role in helping us stay healthy.

Fiber can be divided into two groups: soluble and insoluble. Most plant foods provide both, but some foods are particularly good sources of one type or the other. *Soluble fiber* (in apples and citrus fruits, barley, legumes, and oats) can help reduce high blood cholesterol levels and control blood sugar levels by slowing down the absorption of sugar. *Insoluble fiber* (in cereals, corn bran, wheat bran, whole-grain breads, and vegetables) speeds the passage of waste material though the body. In this way it helps to prevent constipation, hemorrhoids, and diverticular disease; it may also protect against bowel cancer.

Recommended guidelines suggest eating 25 grams or more of fiber daily (about two times the current intake levels in the U.S.).

Food Guide Pyramid This guide is an outline of what to eat daily in order to follow the Dietary Guidelines for Americans. The Pyramid is based on the U.S. Department of Agriculture's research on what Americans eat, what nutrients are in these foods, and how to make the best food choices. *(See also Pyramid, pages 6 and 7.)*

Free radicals These highly reactive molecules can cause damage to cell walls and DNA (the genetic material found within cells). They are believed to be involved in the development of heart disease, some cancers, and premature aging. The body naturally produces free radicals; but certain factors, such as cigarette smoke, pollution, and overexposure to sunlight, can accelerate their production.

Glycemic Index (GI) This is used to measure the rate that carbohydrates are digested and converted into sugar (glucose and glycogen) to raise blood sugar levels and provide energy. Foods with a high GI are quickly broken down and offer an immediate energy boost; those with a lower GI are absorbed more slowly, making you feel full longer and helping to keep blood sugar levels constant. High-GI foods include sugar, honey, and watermelon. Low-GI foods include dried apricots, cherries, pears, whole-grain cereals, and pasta. *(See also Couscous, page 82.)*

Minerals These inorganic substances perform a wide range of vital functions. The *macrominerals*— calcium, chloride, magnesium, potassium, sodium, and sulfur — are present and needed in the largest amounts by the body. Trace minerals, or *microminerals,* are present in the body in amounts less than 5 grams and include chromium, copper, iron, selenium, and zinc.

There are important differences in the body's ability to absorb minerals from different foods, which can be affected by the presence of other substances. For example, oxalic acid, present in spinach, interferes with the absorption of much of the iron and calcium that spinach contains.

• *Calcium* is essential for the development of strong bones and teeth. It also plays an important role in blood clotting. Good sources include dairy products, canned fish (eaten with their bones), and dark green leafy vegetables.

• *Chloride* helps to maintain the body's fluid balance. The main source in the diet is table salt.

• *Chromium* is important in the regulation of blood sugar levels. Good dietary sources include unrefined foods, especially liver, brewer's yeast, whole grains, nuts, and cheeses.

• *Copper*, a component of many enzymes, is needed for bone growth and the formation of connective tissue. It helps the body absorb iron from food. Good sources include seafood, nuts, grains, seeds and legumes.

• *Iron* is an essential component of hemoglobin, the pigment in red blood cells that carries oxygen around the body. Good sources include eggs, fish, legumes, meats, nuts, poultry, whole grain and enriched breads and cereals, and some dried fruits such as dried apricots.

• *Magnesium* is important for healthy bones, the release of energy from food, and nerve and muscle function. Good sources include chocolate, cocoa, dark green leafy vegetables, legumes, nuts, seafood, and whole grains.

• *Potassium*, along with sodium, is important in maintaining the balance of fluid in the body and regulating blood pressure. It is also essential for the transmission of nerve impulses. Good sources include fruit, especially bananas and citrus fruits, legumes, nuts, potatoes, and seeds.

• *Selenium* is a powerful antioxidant that protects cells against damage by free radicals. Good sources include grains, meats, and seafood.

• *Sodium* works with potassium to regulate fluid balance, and is essential for nerve and muscle function. Only a little sodium is needed; we tend to get too much in our diet. The main source in the diet is table salt, as well as salty processed foods and ready-prepared foods.

• *Sulfur* is a part of the essential amino acid methionine, as well as two B vitamins, thiamine and biotin. All protein-containing foods, such as eggs, fish, legumes, meats, milk, nuts, and poultry, are good sources.

• *Zinc* is part of many enzymes and is associated with insulin. It is also involved in the transport of vitamin A and in taste perception. Good sources include protein-containing foods, such as eggs, liver, meat, seafood (especially oysters), as well as whole-grain cereals.

Phytochemicals Found in most plant foods, these biologically active compounds are believed to be beneficial in disease prevention. Among the literally thousands, here are a few:

• *Allicin*, a phytochemical found in garlic, onions, leeks, chives, and shallots, is believed to help lower high blood cholesterol levels and stimulate the immune system.

• *Bioflavonoids* are compounds that provide the yellow and orange colors in fruits and vegetables. They act as antioxidants and are believed to reduce the risk of cancer and heart disease. Three of the more popular bioflavonoids include *quercetin*, *rutin*, and *hesperidin*. Some of the best food sources include apricots, blackberries, dark cherries, plums, and rose hips.

• *Carotenoids*, the best known of which are *beta-carotene* and *lycopene*, are powerful antioxidants thought to help protect us against certain types of cancer. Highly colored fruits and vegetables are excellent sources of carotenoids, such as black currants, carrots, mangoes, sweet potatoes, pumpkin, tomatoes, and dark green leafy vegetables.

• *Glucosinolates*, found mainly in cruciferous vegetables, particularly broccoli, Brussels sprouts, cabbage, cauliflower, and kale, are believed to have strong anti-cancer effects. *Sulforaphane* is one of the powerful cancer-fighting substances produced by glucosinolates.

• *Phytoestrogens* have a chemical structure similar to the female hormone estrogen. They are believed to help protect against hormone-related cancers, such as breast and prostate cancer. One type of phytochemical, called *isoflavone*, may help to relieve symptoms associated with menopause. Soybeans are a particularly rich source of isoflavones.

Protein This nutrient is necessary for growth and development, for maintenance and repair of cells, and for the production of enzymes, antibodies, and hormones. It is essential to keep the body working efficiently. Protein is made up of *amino acids*, compounds which contain the four elements necessary for life: carbon, hydrogen, oxygen, and nitrogen. We need all twenty amino acids commonly found in plant and animal proteins. The human body can make eleven, but the remaining nine—called *essential amino acids*—must be obtained from food.

Protein comes in a wide variety of foods. Dairy products, eggs, fish, meat, and soybeans contain all of the essential amino acids, and are called *complete proteins*. Cereals, legumes, nuts, and seeds are also good sources of protein, but they lack one or more of the essential amino acids, so they are referred to as *incomplete proteins*. If you include a variety of protein foods in your diet, both from animal and plant sources, your body will get all the amino acids it needs. It is important to eat protein foods every day, because the body cannot store essential amino acids for later use. The recommended intake level is 50 grams in a 2,000 calorie diet.

Vitamins Organic compounds essential for good health, vitamins are required in only small amounts. Each vitamin performs specific vital functions. Since the human body cannot make most vitamins, they must be obtained from the diet. The body is capable of storing some vitamins (A, D, and E) and reabsorbing B_{12}. The remaining vitamins need to be provided by the diet on a regular basis. A well-balanced diet, containing a wide variety of different foods, is the best way to get all the vitamins you need. Vitamins can be divided into two groups: *water-soluble* (B complex and C) and *fat-soluble* (A, D, and E). Water-soluble vitamins are easily destroyed during cooking, preparing, processing, and storing food. Fat-soluble vitamins are less vulnerable to losses by cooking and processing.

• *Vitamin A* (retinol) is essential for healthy vision, eyes, skin, and growth. Good sources include butter, cheese, cream, eggs, fortified margarine, fortified milk, and liver. The body can convert *beta-carotene*, the yellow-orange pigment found in many colored fruits and vegetables, into vitamin A. In addition to acting as a source of vitamin A, beta-carotene plays an important role as an antioxidant in the body. The best sources of beta-carotene include broccoli, spinach and other dark green leafy vegetables, deep orange fruits (apricots and cantaloupe), and vegetables (carrots, squash, and sweet potatoes).

• *The B Complex vitamins* have very similar roles to play in nutrition, and many of them occur together in the same foods.

Vitamin B_1 (thiamine) is essential in the release of energy from carbohydrates. The best sources include legumes, liver, whole-grain or enriched breads and cereals, nuts, and pork products.

Vitamin B_2 (riboflavin) is vital for growth, healthy skin and eyes, and helps release energy from food. Good sources include cottage cheese, meat, milk, leafy green vegetables, whole-grain or enriched breads and cereals, and yogurt.

Niacin (nicotinic acid), sometimes called vitamin B_3, plays an important role in releasing energy within the cells. Unlike the other B vitamins, the body can make niacin from the essential amino acid *tryptophan*. Good sources include eggs, fish, meats, milk, poultry, whole-grain and enriched breads and cereals, nuts, and all protein-containing foods.

Vitamin B_6 (pyridoxine) helps the body to utilize protein and contributes to the formation of hemoglobin for red blood cells. B_6 is found in fish, fruits, whole grains, legumes, poultry, shellfish, and green leafy vegetables.

Vitamin B_{12} (cyanocobalamin) is vital for growth, the formation of red blood cells, and maintenance of a healthy nervous system. B_{12} is unique in that it is only found in foods of animal origin. Vegetarians who eat dairy products will get enough, but vegans need to include foods fortified with B_{12} in their diet. Good sources of B_{12} include animal products such as cheese, eggs, fish, meat, milk, poultry, and shellfish.

Folate (folic acid) is used in DNA synthesis and is important in the formation of new cells. Folate is important in preventing neural tube defects, such as spina bifida and anencephaly; thus the Public Health Service recommends all women of childbearing age who are capable of becoming pregnant take 0.4 milligrams, or 400 micrograms, of folate daily. As a result, the FDA has mandated that grain products be fortified with folate. The recommended folate level can easily be met by eating 5 or more servings of fruits and vegetables daily, especially leafy green vegetables and oranges. Other good sources include legumes, liver, and seeds.

• *Vitamin C* (ascorbic acid) is essential for growth and vital for the formation of collagen (a protein needed for healthy bones, teeth, gums, blood capillaries, and all connective tissue). It plays an important role in the healing of wounds and fractures, and acts as a powerful antioxidant. The best sources include citrus fruits, cabbage, cantaloupe, lettuce, mangoes, papayas, peppers, strawberries, and dark green vegetables.

• *Vitamin D* (cholecalciferol) is essential for the growth and absorption of calcium, and thus for the formation of healthy bones. Upon exposure to sunlight, the body can synthesize vitamin D. Good food sources include fortified products such as butter, cereals, margarine, and milk.

• *Vitamin E* is not just one vitamin, but a number of related compounds called tocopherols, which function as antioxidants. Good sources of polyunsaturated plant oils and their products include margarine, mayonnaise, salad dressings, and shortenings, plus egg yolks, fortified cereals, liver, nuts, seeds (especially sunflower seeds) leafy green vegetables, and whole-grain products.

glossary

141

Index

  Page numbers in italicized type refer to photographs or illustrations.